Penguin Education

The Forsaken Lover
White Words and Black People
Chris Searle

Chris Searle studied English at the University of Leeds
and at McMaster University, Ontario. He then taught
in Canada before going to Tobago, as an English teacher
in a secondary school (1968–9). His experience there
forms the basis of *The Forsaken Lover*. When he
returned to the United Kingdom, he taught in Stepney,
and was one of the editors of *Stepney Words*. He is also
the author of *Poilu* (Workshop Press, 1971), *This New Season*
(Calder & Boyars, 1973) and editor of a national anthology
of children's poetry, *Fire Words* (Cape, 1972). He is a
member of the Rank and File Socialist Teacher's Group
within the National Union of Teachers.

The Forsaken Lover
White Words and Black People
Chris Searle

Penguin Books

Penguin Books Ltd, Harmondsworth,
Middlesex, England
Penguin Books Australia Ltd,
Ringwood, Victoria, Australia

First published by Routledge & Kegan Paul 1972
Published by Penguin Books 1973
Copyright © Chris Searle, 1972

All royalties from the sale of this book
will be paid to an arts trust in Tobago

Made and printed in Great Britain by
Hazell Watson & Viney Ltd,
Aylesbury, Bucks
Set in Linotype Times

To the children of Tobago,
who began my education

Contents

Preface to Penguin edition

Today I read in the newspapers about the 'blacking' of container lorries in London and Liverpool. I read of the 'black' and horrific conflict in Ulster. A few weeks ago I read that I had been 'blacklisted' by a body of headmasters in East London. In yesterday's paper I read the words of a High Court judge, who spoke from his bench in appalled dignity, about the 'denigration' of the National Industrial Relations Court, and last week I read a statement of the President of the newly formed National Union of School Students: 'We must win the right to be respected as individuals. We are denigrated to the point where we can be even caned at will by the headmaster.'

'Black' has gone far beyond a word merely representing a colour. Whether we use the common English 'black' or 'to blacken', or words from Latin roots having similar connotations, like the verb 'to denigrate', to indicate meanings like 'bad', 'evil', 'unworthy', or 'to defame', we are perpetuating through our daily use of language the insults and disrespect the white world has always heaved upon the black man. The Oxford English Dictionary says as much about man's inhumanity to man, and the complex and insidious ways in which the white world has dominated and mystified the black, as any history book or political tract. Some of the meanings and associations given to the word 'black' in the Concise Oxford Dictionary (widely used in the schools) are:

deadly, sinister, wicked, hateful,
dismal, threatening, implying disgrace
or condemnation, discredited, corrupt.

We speak our words in a white world which vindicates and congratulates everything white through its language and symbolism, while simultaneously denying, debasing and 'denigrating' everything black. When this denial of blackness takes place daily in the schools through language 'development', we are conditioned to stifle and forget consciousness of the social racism propagated through the symbolic meanings of the English language's use of 'black' and 'white'. It is hardly surprising that within the black man's demands for a re-definition of his identity, there is also a massive need to re-define the meanings of words and symbols that still reflect and give support to a colonial, racist world. The same Oxford Dictionary has these meanings and associations under the word 'white':

innocent, unstained, of harmless kind,
integrity, person of honourable character,
good breeding, clean appearance.

The English language has its roots in a savage historical racism and pride. The white man devised a language based on words and symbols which protected himself and advertised his belief in the primacy of his colour. When he promotes that language to a non-white people, it is a way of breaking apart the identity of those people, dividing them from themselves and subjecting them to the white values and political thinking which are assimilated and spoken out through that language. And the white 'values' and thinking of the nations which have been the strongest colonial powers – Britain, France, the United States of America, Portugal, Holland – were, and still are the 'values' and thinking of capitalism.

When 'black' is used so constantly and unwittingly by people as a word of debasement, even by young student militants or the militant working class in their terms of industrial action, we must shout out a redefinition of the word and its associations. We must also work towards developing a new consciousness of the ideas of black and white in the schools, through a continuous questioning and scrutiny of the origins of the symbols we use in the language, which inculcate into our black and white children the seeds of alienation, hate and despair. Through this poem, for example, a fifteen-year-old East London girl began to question and undermine some of the traditional linguistic bigotry of the language:

Black and white

I'm white, he's black –
   is it so bad?
Or is it what people say?
   They can say some
     nasty things
      I know
     I've heard them.
  Why can't they leave us alone?
It's our lives, we'll do what we want.
  But if he was white,
    well . . .
  that would be different
   'He's one of us,
    not them.'
  Why can't they just
    try
  and see it our way?
  We can't help it,
    It's not that bad,
    It's not his fault
     he's black.
    Nor is it our fault
     we're white.

The struggles for black freedom in America, or through West Indian voices like those of Marcus Garvey, Frantz Fanon and Walter Rodney, and the black presses in this country like New Beacon Books and Bogle-L'Ouverture Publications, have meant that there is a new meaning in the English language for the word 'black'. 'Black man' is 'one who struggles, one who fights oppression'. In this sense, with this meaning, we should all be black:

Black power
Yes, Black power
The owners of the world
Black the creators of the world
Black the white
White the black
The creators
Black the humans

Fourteen-year-old boy
Stepney
July 1972

Acknowledgements

The authors and publishers wish to thank the following for permission to reproduce the works cited, or extracts from them:

Oxford University Press for the extracts from *Rights of Passage and Islands* by Edward Brathwaite.

Jonathan Cape Ltd for extract from 'Laventille', *The Castaway*, by Derek Walcott.

Farrar, Straus & Giroux Inc. for extract from *The Gulf* by Derek Walcott, copyright © 1963, 1964, 1965, 1969, 1970 by Derek Walcott.

Basil Smith for *The Church*.

Marguerite Wyke for *History Leaves No Memorials to the Poor*.

All possible care has been taken to trace ownership of extracts in the volume and to make full acknowledgement of their use.

Introduction

My first impulse is to question my authority in writing and compiling this book. I am dealing with perhaps the most sprawling and amorphous of concepts, and I am writing about children who wear a different skin to mine and experience a completely different society and environment. I am a foreigner, an Englishman from the London suburbs discussing the education of black children in a Caribbean island. The situation is absurd enough to begin with, even though I spent a year among them as an English teacher in a secondary school in Tobago. A knowledge of one's own identity is something each individual spends a lifetime in chasing in the context of his fellows. I can only say that from what I have seen and read, the West Indian probably has a greater problem of identity than most other people. In Tobago and the Windward Islands he is predominantly ex-African, his ancestors shoved on to a Caribbean island by white traders perhaps three centuries ago; he is displaced to an extent that only he knows.

> We left
> somewhere a life we never found,
>
> customs and gods that are not born again,
> some crib, some grill of light
> clanged shut on us in bondage, and withheld
>
> us from that world below us and beyond,
> and in its swaddling cerements we're still bound.[1]

My first slim experience teaching West Indian children in England suggests to me that the statements made in this work on language and alienation apply to them perhaps with even greater force. They have moved towards a further degree of displacement. As English people they may find a new identity. As English people with black skins speaking English in England, they have a new identity which may speak against them if their teachers are not wary.

It is with these thoughts and cautions that I write this account, more as editor and commentator than critic, with the feeling that at as many times as possible, words of West Indian, child and man, shall speak out for themselves. Their experience is far more valid than any objective notion that I can claim to make: 'I have not wished to be objective. Besides, that would be dishonest. It is not possible for me to be objective. . . . Why not quite the simple attempt to touch the other, to feel the other, to explain the other to myself?'[2]

As new nations emerge, and struggle against a colonial legacy and previous structures of domination, the issue of 'identity' becomes a conscious and anxious preoccupation for their peoples. 'Who am I?' 'What is this place?' 'Who are these people around me?' 'Do I belong to these people?' These are all questions that loom suddenly out of the phlegmatic acceptance of the old order. A notion of identity involves the connection and sympathy a man feels with himself, and the people and places around him that are built into his world, with a feeling of belongingness in that world, that a man's special uniqueness has a definite place there.

A culture, said E. H. Erikson, must 'provide an early basis' for the identity of a child. He needs to feel, as he grows towards adolescence, that there is a structure of 'meaningful wider belongingness'[3] behind his relationship with himself and his family, some supporting social strength in which he can trust. In addition to this fundamental need, the West Indian child has to integrate his own life-cycle within the upheaval of the changing state of his country's political identity as it becomes a disparate political entity – an island nation. He may be a West Indian abroad, but at home he is a Trinidadian, a Grenadian, a St Lucian. Even in an uneasy unity between two islands like Trinidad and Tobago, a Trinidadian is still a Trinidadian and a Tobagonian still a Tobagonian. But as these new, separate nations find their independent political identities, their people still speak in a language that takes them back to the past and their subjection and exploitation through centuries of slavery and colonialism. They also inevitably retain many of the old forms: their skins tell of Africa and Asia, their religions of Canterbury and Rome, the political institutions of Europe and America. Their economies are shackled by the banks and interests of New York, Canada and London, and their education system speaks of Oxford and Cambridge Examination Boards. And they live on islands, some only a few miles from the South American coast. Their language speaks against them and tells them that 'black' is a bad word, a word of guilt and doubt and evil, but that 'white' has its associations with purity, goodness and innocence. Their old identity was one of limitation, subservience and alienation, cutting them off from themselves and their own dignity. Their new identity must speak of them and their own world, for their own ideas and standards, their language and their art.

We find our identities through our language. That language must uphold us, give us confidence, tell us we belong to our world and each other. If our world is an island, it must make our island ours, not dissipate it to an alien mass and leave us a void. It is our language that provides us with the particular dominant national images that sustain our particular culture, and build the structure of belongingness and trust that most people need, giving to the individual self the ability to experience the necessary social sense of continuity and sameness. A man becomes absurd when his language divides him from his world, divorces him from his surroundings and his fellows, and makes him speak of foreign things. It is his language that forges out and articulates his images of identity: 'One uses the language which helps to preserve one's life, which helps to make one feel at peace with the world, and which screens out the greatest amount of chaos.'[4]

But in the European language of the Caribbean black man there is disorder and chaos. It is the disorder of mimicry. The language tenses with the nature. The words and images mock the man who speaks and feels them. He covers himself with foreignness. 'Nothing is more astonishing than to hear a black man express himself properly, for then in truth he is putting on a white world ... he is a complete replica of the white man. So there is nothing to do but give in.'[5]

1 Monostatus

The reader of this work is urged to read the testament of Frantz Fanon in his *Black Skin White Masks*. It is the most powerful statement on the Caribbean black man's problem of identity and struggles with the white world that I have read. While I was reading it, I found myself saying, 'I must quote all this book. This man has felt and known and *is* everything I have to say. It is all inside him.' From his book, Fanon heaves himself and his blackness at the reader, giving him another, separate existence. I found myself turning to his work after I had written my own account, and his words and insights seemed to be what I had been struggling to find by being amongst others with a different coloured skin from mine. What I have to say comes from outside a black skin, based on my experience with others. Fanon speaks from inside blackness, based on his experience as himself. His statements crystallize, from a man's own existence on another island, what I have to say from my own:

We understand now why the black man cannot take pleasure in his insularity. For him there is only one way out, and it leads into the white world.

Every colonized people – in other words, every people in whose soul an inferiority complex has been created by the death and burial of its local cultural originality – finds itself face to face with the language of the civilizing nation, that is, with the culture of the mother country.

Willy-nilly, the [Caribbean] Negro has to wear the livery that the white world has sewed for him.

White civilization and European culture have forced an existential deviation on the Negro.

Imprisoned on his island, lost in the atmosphere that offers not the slightest outlet, the Negro breathes in the appeal of Europe like pure air.[1]

The same day that I was reading *Black Skins White Masks*. I went in the evening to see *The Magic Flute* by Mozart. I knew very little about the opera, and nothing about the story. I think that I was still thinking about Fanon. Then the overture and the first scene: the flowing beauty, the order of the sounds – the artifice of genius. 'But what is this now? A black man on the stage? What is he doing here?' Ah, 'Monostatus, a negro in the service of Sarastro.' But look how he moves like a clown. Look how the white man who plays him gives him all his ridicule. Look how he makes his eyes roll. Look how he ogles the white, pure heroine and now tries to rape her. Look how the fool in feathers calls him the devil. Look how he is pulled off the stage to be whipped by some white men. Look how he grovels at the feet of his white master, the epitome of wisdom, enlightenment and truth. Listen how his master tells him, 'Your soul is as black as your face.' Look how he falls down into darkness and punishment like the other evil characters at the end of the play. All in Mozart, all within the forms and moulds of art and beauty, all inside the same time and same day as Fanon's open soul.

Then there *is* more to be said. The thing must be said again, and again. We take school parties of our children to see *The Magic Flute*, and Fanon is still almost an unknown name, just a vague scare of blackness. We laugh at the grotesque Monostatus, the black bogey man, and applaud the white world of art that his distorted shape fits into. It still suits us to remember him that way. We do not want to know the black man. We do not want to climb inside him. We would rather have our fools and caricatures and hoist them in the name of beauty, tradition and myth. We turn our back on real men, real existence, real blackness. We do not want to read and experience Fanon:

I cannot go to a film without seeing myself. I wait for me.
In the interval, just before the film starts, I wait for me.
The people in the theatre are watching me, examining
me, waiting for me. A Negro groom is going to appear.
My heart makes my head swim.[2]

But what to do with Monostatus? He is a legend and a funny black sheep that we and our children accept and laugh at, and soon enough we extend feelings for the myth to cover the reality. Then what do we say to ourselves and our children? That he isn't really as foolish as Monostatus? That it was the ignorance of the Age of Reason that has been passed down to us and perpetuates itself in us? What if the children we tell are black themselves? How do we explain this sudden distortion of their own existence?

The Little Black Boy

My mother bore me in the southern wild,
And I am black, but O! my soul is white;
White as an angel is the English child,
But I am black, as if bereav'd of light.

My mother taught me underneath a tree,
And sitting down before the heat of day,
She took me on her lap and kissed me,
And pointing to the east, began to say:

'Look on the rising sun: there God does live,
And gives his light, and gives his heat away;
And flowers and trees and beasts and men receive
Comfort in morning, joy in the noonday

And we are put on earth a little space,
That we may learn to bear the beams of love:
And these black bodies and this sunburnt face
Is but a cloud, and like a shady grove.

For when our souls have learn'd the heat to bear,
The cloud will vanish: we shall hear his voice,
Saying: "Come out of the grove, my love and care,
And round my golden tent like lambs rejoice".'

Thus did my mother say, and kissed me;
And thus I say to little English boy.
When I from black and he from white cloud free,
And round the tent of God like lambs we joy,

I'll shade him from the heat, till he can bear
To lean in joy upon our father's knee;
And then I'll stand and stroke his silver hair,
And be like him, and he will then love me.

William Blake, another eighteenth-century white man, in a 'song of innocence' gives a statement of blackness. The black boy feels guilty about his blackness. He can only see himself in relation to the white world, and the white 'angelic' child. So he must convince the world that, despite the black-ness of his skin, his soul is white and pure. The eternal part of him must be white, he says. His blackness is only a cover, only a cloud to evaporate when he dies, to reveal his beauti-ful white soul beneath. Christian symbolism has always venerated whiteness; the dove, the lamb, the robe, the white brightness of purity and holiness. 'God is light', only the evil is dark. Christianity, essentially and historically a white man's religion, is built on the vindication of whiteness and white symbols. Consequently it has been used as an emotive weapon to enslave and degrade the black man. English children still write in each others' autograph books:

God made the little black boys
He made them in the night
He made them in a hurry
And forgot to paint them white.

The Church was very effective in the vanguard of colonial-ism: no black Christian proselyte wanted a black soul. Christianity seemed to give the possibility of becoming white, eternally white: in the next world. It offered black skins, white souls. Blake's poem is a symptom of the insidiousness of the white man's symbolism, built as it is on the positivism of white and the negativism of black, the rightness and dignity of white and the wrongness and degradation of black. The white God gives his light to the black man, bestowing his power in the name of truth. The sun rises in the east, but for the black mother and child it rises over Europe:

Look on the rising sun: there God does live,
And gives his light, and gives his heat away . . .

The white heat of power and subjection is accepted by the mother as beams of love from the white God. These must be endured. The black mother urges acceptance, stoicism to her son: their blackness will eventually and providentially pass away, and they will step out good and white from their shady grove in the southern wild, to play with the white children and stroke their silvery, flowing hair. Then the white children will love the little black boy. As long as he becomes white in mind and belief, throws off his blackness and worships at the white altar, shades the white boy from the sun and idolizes his hair texture, he will be accepted by the white boy. But only as long as he promises to be white:

And be like him, and he will then love me.

Until he becomes white he is unacceptable, even in the eyes of the white man's God. He will only find acceptance as idolater of the white boy's whiteness, saving him from the heat, envying his white beauty with fondling and stroking of the white boy's hair. To the white world, the black boy can only find identity in terms of submission and service to the white way of life. This is the identity that the black boy learns through the white man's language, schools and churches, and it is an identity that embitters and alienates him.

The little black boy is different now. He has a new view of his mother, his history and himself. He sees the domina-

tion of white and the role of the white man's church in
keeping him unaware of the rightness of his blackness. In
1970 he is very angry about these things:

The Church

It was here
by the wall of the
little white church
a young black mother,
her belly big
with child and
future generations,
was eaten down
to pulp
by the chattering
shells of a Thompson automatic.
Their pure, red blood
soaked the building
to its festering foundations.

More,
many more of us
died
within the walls
of this gateway to deliverance
which stands at the heart
of our village,
the sum total of Europe's generosity.
The soil on which
it sits
being but dust in the eye
of her greed.

Now,
We wrap the bodies in
the music of goat-skins
and lift our voices
to a God so fearsome,
He has but one cheek.

Basil Smith[3]

Blake's 1789 'Song of Innocence' was a poem about how a black mother educated her child. The mother's voice of experience urged stoicism to the child: accept the life on earth, and the slave identity which comes with it. In 1971 there is *Soledad Brother*, also about education. George Jackson educated himself from his own experience, the journey of his own consciousness as he became more and more aware of his wounded identity as a black man in a white world. His education in prison involved the unlearning of the white man's view of the black man, pushed into him by his formal schooling and his mother's protectiveness. In prison his education was a war with himself and his own identity as a black American: 'the greatest battle is with oneself'. Like Blake's black child, Jackson had his first education from his mother: the education for acceptance and survival. From prison he wrote to his mother that 'experience has made me better informed', and his real education through experience and awareness forms a gradual rejection of his mother's advice:

If I followed the advice I receive it would only serve to enslave me further to this madness of our times . . . .

I feel that you have failed me, Mama. I know that you have failed me.

The little Black Boy did not turn round to his mother and answer

I've been alone for a long time. This is why I've had so much pain and trouble. . . . You gave me god and that horrible church. Even god managed to take something away from me. I have nothing left but myself.[4]

Soledad Brother is a poem of experience. It is what the child shouts back at the mother when he begins to know his world:

Why did you allow us to worship at a white altar? Why even now, following tragedy after tragedy, crisis after crisis, do you still send Jon to that school where he is taught to feel inferior, and why do you continue to send

me Easter cards? This is the height of disrespect you
show me. You never wanted me to be a man nor Jon
neither. You don't want us to defeat our enemies. What
is wrong with you, Mama? No other mama in History
has acted the way you act under stress situations.

I won't be a good *boy* ever.

The dancing lamb is the fighting panther, the white idolator
becomes the white destroyer. There is no delight for the
black boy in enjoying the white life as a subjected, fawning
companion of the white child. Blake's black child was an
alienated child. His skin is black, but his eyes and mind are
set on white. He looks towards the white world and white
children and only sees himself imperfect, incomplete, 'bereav'd'. Jackson's eyes were on himself, his black brothers,
his freedom. The white world only left him 'alienated and
isolated'.

Now these four statements come from black children in
England trapped in a white situation, surrounded by white
groups. Like Jackson, they all express alienation and
isolation:

There all alone
isolated and contaminated
where no one speaks
nor hears what you say
They talk about how
you dress and how
you speak
if I ever speak.
No one to talk to
No one no one

One day a stranger
knocked on the door
I opened the door
for loneliness had gone
but then the bills man
enters in with a scorn

on his face and full of sin.
Out on the street again
was met with loneliness
again with no one
No one

Walking about the street with my hands in pocket,
nobody really cares about me. My only true friend is the
black suit I always wear, which I've had for years. People
walk about in groups, all gay and laughing, while me, I
walk all alone in my old black suit. Suddenly I see
someone coming to me, a bunch of boys and girls. How
happy I felt. Then it all disappeared again and left me
lonely.

I am very lonely Nowhere to go
Nowhere to play, not a friend
To share my grief only myself.

When the sun shines I go outside
and play with my shadow
But yet it cannot do me much
as if I had a friend.

Sometimes when I am dreaming I dream
of how I play with a lot of girls
But just as I get up it all go away

Sometimes I say to myself I wish I could
sleep and dream of friends
and that my dreams will never
                              ends

I dreamed that I was riding on a bicycle and I was going
to crash into a wall and the brakes would not work. Then
something hooked me and I was stuck in the air. I looked
to see who hooked me. I saw nothing. I unhooked myself
and went inside a house to see who hooked me. It was a
fairly big house, and I looked in all the rooms. I saw a
big cupboard that had been left by the owners. I opened
it and there were two boys. I said, 'I will not hurt you.'

They rushed past me and ran as fast as they could. I
never saw them again.

Many children feel alone in claustrophobic city surroundings, the environment of these particular children. But there
is a haunting consistency in these statements, the loneliness
of the children somehow has a similar pitch throughout. One
waits inside her house, 'isolated and contaminated', one
wanders down the street with her old black suit which she
always wears, one plays with her shadow, another walks
through an empty house. They are all forsaken. In each case
other children seem to be coming to relieve the loneliness,
as if the child has expectations of comfort and company,
but they always fade away, sometimes sharply, sometimes
slowly. And there is the sense that the black child himself
accepts the guilt for the disappearance. White children too
can sense this aloneness and forsakenness of the black child
in the white world:

The little girl stood alone
I wondered why?
The white kids called her names
I wondered why?
Then I realized . . . she was a coloured child

She looked the same to me
It seemed all wrong
She even talked in a London way
It was all wrong
But then . . . she was a coloured child

And:

Alone he walks
He walks alone
He has no friends
And has no home
I noticed something from the back
He is alone because he's black.

Or:

The Immigrant

He walks down the lonely street
With a pair of old shoes on his feet.
A job he cannot find,
People say they're a different kind.

They look and point in the street
And they talk about the things they eat.
They come to England to make a career
But people just stop and sneer.

Why? He's your brother
You should treat him like you
Treat your mother.

Or there is the feeling that the white children will speak
and play only out of conscience or patronage:

I live in a block of flats where people
do play I have no friends day after day
if I have no friend I can't play
so I stay in and look after myself

I noticed they started to talk to
Me it was because I was black
and they were just saying to theirselves, let's speak
Don't be rotten

These children speak of the same terrifying alienation and
self-condemnation that the little Black Boy was told by his
mother to accept, and which George Jackson rejected and
fought up to the last moment of his life, loving his blackness:

I think only of how I live, how well, how nobly. We think
if we are to be men again we must stop working for
nothing, competing against each other for the little they
allow us to possess, stop selling our women or allowing
them to be used and handled against their will, stop

letting our children be educated by the barbarian, using
their language, dress and customs, and most assuredly
stop turning our cheeks.

The 'innocence' of Blake's little Black Boy is the mystified
innocence of black children in England, America, the
Caribbean, or in any land where the English have ruled and
the English language is spoken by black people. But the lost
blackness, the lost identity is being looked for again and
being found. Black children, whether they are in a neo-
colonial situation like Trinidad and Tobago, or an immigrant situation like England, now have the power and the
growing awareness to be conscious of their loss. They are
beginning to go on a journey to recover it, like a child who
has lost the most treasured part of himself:

On Friday 9.30 a.m.
I heard a kitten cry
I went looking for it
It was in a tree across a river
I wondered how it got there.
So I swam across
but it was no good
the current was drawing me away
I wish I was in a boat
Then I was shouting for help
no one heard me
I was just going over then I fainted
when I woke up the dock attendant said
'I saved your life'
so I thanked him and said,
'I have to be on my way
I am going to save a kitten.'
'Where is it?
What colour is it?'
'It is black,' I said.
'You nearly died for that kitten.'
Then he said,
'It was my kitten it always goes up there.'

So then he sat down and cried.
I said
'Don't cry.'

Our children and ourselves must break the old mythology. As the black man smashes the icons of Monostatus and the little Black Boy, he is destroying parts of our own ignorance, and we must be with him, not against him. Our friendships and our children are more important than the caricatures and myths that we set up about others for the sake of our own pride and power. Fanon only asks for something that we all hope: 'that the tool never possess the man. That the enslavement of man by man cease forever ... That it may be possible for me to discover and love man, wherever he may be.'[5]

2 The island theme

On the bank of this brook, I found many pleasant
savana's or meadows, plain, smooth and cover'd with
grass; and on the rising parts of them next to the higher
grounds, where the water, as it might be supposed, never
overflow'd, I found a great deal of tobacco, green, and
growing to a great and very strong stalk. . . . I came to an
opening, where the country seem'd to descend to the
west, and a little spring of fresh water, which issued
out of the side of the hill by me, run the other way, that
is, due east; and the country appear'd so fresh, so green,
so flourishing, everything being in a constant verdure or
flourish of spring, that it looked like a planted garden.
I descended a little on the side of that delicious vale,
surveying it with a secret kind of pleasure (tho' mixt
with other afflicting thoughts) to think that this was all
my own, that I was king and lord of all this country
indefeasibly, and had a right of possession; and if I could
convey it, I might have it in inheritance as compleatly
as any lord of a manor in England. I saw here abundance
of cocoa trees, orange and lemon, and citron trees; but
all wild and very few bearing any fruit, at least not then.
However, the green limes that I gathered were not only
pleasant to eat, but very wholesome; and I mix'd their
juice afterwards with water, which made it very
wholesome, and very cool and refreshing.

Defoe, *Robinson Crusoe*

Advantages of living on an island are, in an island their
will not be much violence, discrimination as in the
countries. In an island the people there will have to
work hard at their jobs whether it is working in a garden
or in a store.

Most of the people there will be hard working people
and when they work for a few cents, all will spend to
feed and clothe a family. Rich people will not mistreat
their servants. If someone is working for some one they
will be treated kindly.

In an island there will be peace and hardly any noise.
The most noise you may here is from the animals playing
in bushes. There will not be many kidnapping many road
deaths and sad scenes.

Children who live on an island will be healthy, cheerful
children, they will be contented and grow up obedient
and hard working in both work and schooling.

On some islands there will be lovely beaches with palm
trees and coconut trees. Most of the trees and shrubs
will be there and an artist could make a good scenery
there. Tourism will go on on an island because there will
be quietness, and peace and thats what tourist likes. They
also come to see the beautiful flowers in bloom.

People will be welcome with hospitality on an island
more than in a city. There will be pleasant smiles and
friendly and cheerful greetings as they pass you. They
won't be much haughtiness and quarels about who has
more money. . . .

Thirteen-year-old girl

The colonizer and decolonized, Crusoe and the child of
Friday, are talking about their island. One asserts possession, the other simply accepts that her island is hers. One
sees produce, fertility and merchandise around him, the
other sees her home and identity, but they both realize that
their lives are concerned with this island, that they have a
link, a relationship with its oneness and its beauty.

English language and poetry have always valued the idea

and image of the Island. It has suggested many themes: man's own isolation, a dream of beauty, a stage to be passed on a journey of life, the sanctuary and retreat, the place of escape. And the world has been an island and the island has been a Paradise – the themes have often been associated with each other. The European mind has often had a strange compulsion to crystallize its myths and dreams in terms of an island, in order to focus them clearly in a distinct and discrete vision. Shakespeare made his 'Theatrum Mundi', his stage of the world, an enchanted island where Caliban scraped in the earth. Crusoe, trapped on his island, surrounded by the apparent conditions of Paradise, worked it into profits. In this century Golding has played out his history of the world on an island, and Huxley ended his vision on one, seeing it snatched away by the powers of commerce and greed. A sixteen-year-old girl writing in an English school sees an island as a mirage:

Bewildered in a wilderness I turned
tormented by the yellow glare of the sun's despair,
To where a long-sought island stood out clear
but turned to dust and air as I drew near.[1]

There has been this reoccurring hope of release to an island, a different, mythical world that the imagination hoists as its ideal. There is Shelley's island; the image of human perfectibility:

Other flowering isles must be
In the sea of Life and Agony:
Other spirits float and flee
O'er that gulf: even now, perhaps,
On some rock the wild wind wraps,
With folded wings they waiting sit
For my bark, to pilot it
To some calm and blooming cove,
Where for me, and those I love,
May a windless bower be built,
Far from passion, pain and guilt,

In a dell mid lawny hills,
Which the wild sea-murmur fills,
And soft sunshine, and the sound
Of old forests echoing round,
And the light and smell divine
Of all flowers that breathe and shine:
We may live so happy there,
That the spirits of the air,
Envying us, may even entice
To our healing Paradise
The polluting multitude.
. . . And the love which heals all strife
Circling, like the breath of life,
All things in that sweet abode
With its own mild brotherhood:
They, not it, would change; and soon
Every sprite beneath the moon
Would repent its envy vain
And the earth grow young again.[2]

But the transcendent vision of the early nineteenth century becomes the tourist seduction-piece of the twentieth.
The vision becomes real, they say, in 'Tranquil Tobago —
Crusoe's Island', the two-week, air-conditioned, all-in Eden,
the island of the rum-punch and the Bird of Paradise:

Here is a gem. The finest beaches imaginable, and all
facilities for water-sports. Enchanting, unspoiled scenery.
Tennis, golf. First-class hotels. This island just takes the
Caribbean Oscar from Grenada by a short head. For
those who do not expect deck-chairs on the beach, a
continual whirl of night-life and fabulous shopping, then
Tobago is incomparable . . . our first impression was
'here at last is a paradise'.[3]

But these are white men's voices. 'To each his own', the
calypsonian announces. An island becomes enough of a
world for those people who permanently live on it:
'Grenada for Grenadians, Barbados for Barbadians,

Jamaica for Jamaicans', and if Tobago has its own paradise, it will be enough for Tobagonians, as well as for those
with dollars enough to come there as tourists:

Your native friend will surely be your host
And show you some of the beauty from coast to coast,
Lovely hotels, lovely beaches, lovely flowers, pretty faces,
It is grand
On this Crusoe-land.
Come le'we go Tobago.
That Paradise found by Robinson Crusoe . . .
Now the whol' world say
Come to Tobago for holiday.[4]

The children of these islands often write of Paradise. They
are surrounded and conditioned by the images of both its
reality and exploitation. They have so often had the idea
heaved upon them by both the traditions and symbols of
their western European colonial education, and the sales
talk of the tourist industry that makes dollars for their
island. Even Columbus on his fourth voyage, sailing below
Trinidad in the narrow channel which separates the island
from Venezuela, sensed that he was approaching somewhere
special: 'For I believe the earthly Paradise lies here, which no
one can enter except by God's leave.'[5] Now, a Grenadian
boy writes of his island, using the same image. Like it was
for Columbus and Crusoe, his island is a gift of Providence:

This world it is a Paradise.
We look at the evergreen trees,
The sky and the deep, blue seas
We see the brilliant sunshine that shines so bright.
And the beautiful stars that glitter at night.
Shall we forget this Paradise?

Another follows a similar theme:

Dear Grenada, land of spice,
To me you are a Paradise . . .

The child develops in this strange elision of genuine response to natural beauty, gullibility to the tourist-trade rhetoric and dream of paradisal perfection. In this context, the world outside his island can become irrelevant to him: his own island becomes his world. The world outside is a different world for him. It is a world of 'continents' and 'cities' and the child may only think of islands. 'What's it like in your island?' the little Tobagonian girl asks the bewildered Canadian tourist, full of the hugeness of his own land and his back strapped up with cameras. To her it is a reasonable question – the world comes to her island and brings its money and its cameras, so it must be the centre, the source of the world. And the sea really is that colour of blue, and the trees that green, and the sand that firm and white. The superficial conditions of the paradisal isle are easily met. But there is also another world inside the beauty:

Disadvantages of living on an island are the schooling their might be bad because on an island a teacher will get less that she gets in a city. There may not be enough money and in bigger cities there are plenty money. Work might be hard to get. Rich people on an island may treat their servants like slaves just because they know they will stay to get money to send their children to school.

Meat and fish may be hard to buy because people on an island will want money to go away to some city and sell the meat at a high price.

Children may have to walk to school because of bad transportation and cars may not be able to travel on roads because of bad roads, muddy areas and stones.

Children may not get enough to eat and drink and may suffer from malnutrition. People may die easily from the lack of medical attention. Doctors may not attend to the people properly because of their not having enough money to pay him . . . .

Thirteen-year-old girl

These are the traps in the paradise, and the anxieties within the garden that make the people reach out from the island world to the outside world, to grasp on to the modernity and the white man's compensations. People wake worried in a clouded paradise:

At the Break of Day

Early in the morning
When the first cock crows,
And the grey morning fills the East
And the fog rises out of the streams:
Some men sleep on,
But some are already awake,
Thoughtful and worried
Of the coming day.

Thirteen-year-old girl

And if you have no money, there are few respites. This Eden still has the curse of work:

The Dawn of a New Day

When the dawn is peeping
and everybody awakes
To see the bright morning star
Just creeping away.

And the chipper of birds in the air,
And the sun just peeps up from the east
with all its fragrant light
To show the world its pleasant face
with all its golden stripes,

Then people start to stir about
With all their daily toils.

Thirteen-year-old girl

There is an awareness that an island is also a place of labour, sadness, hurricanes and death, where people have lived in total subjection and slavery. There are the prevail-

ing undercurrents of suffering coming through the children's
words. The clichés of the gay, dancing, uninhibited West
Indian have often been used by the white man to protect his
own conscience. Tobagonian children, considering Heming-
way's *Indian Camp* as a boy's first discovery of the secrets of
life and death, will quickly point out that the young Nick
needs to get into a boat and be rowed to an island in order to
learn of the intensity of these things. They happen in a
special way on an island, they say, there is a special knowledge to be gained there, as if these realities can be seen with
more clarity and meaning there, and the child and artist who
live on an island will both sense that. It is in this sense that
both will see their islands as complete entities, as separate
stages of the world.

3 Language and identity

In V. S. Naipaul's story *A Flag on the Island*, Blackwhite, the black writer, rails about the language problem on his island:

'You know Frankie, I begin to feel that what is wrong with my books is not me, but the language I use. You know, in English, black is a damn bad word. You talk of a black deed. How then can I write in this language?'

'I have told you already. You are getting too black for me.'

'What we want is our own language. I intend to write in our own language. You know the patois we have. Not English, not French, but something we have made up. This is our own. You were right. Damn those lords and ladies. Damn Jane Austen. This is ours, this is what we have to work with.'[1]

His indignation is understandable: his identity is suffering. Language itself is the strongest bridge to a secure identity. A feeling that people speak the same language and have the same words for shared ideas is the integrating force amongst them that gives them the feeling of belongingness and trust that society must radiate. A strong, integrating, common language gives the 'social health' that Erikson concerns himself with in his book *Childhood and Society* – a wide faith in the forms and images of society. But when children have a common language that is held to be an inferior one, or a language whose own words and images divide the child from himself, speak against his skin and assert his own subservience, then that same language becomes the destroyer of his identity and the destroyer of his experience. In R. D. Laing's words: 'The choice of syntax and vocabulary are political acts that define and circumscribe the manner in which "facts" are to be experienced. Indeed, in a sense they go further and even create the facts that are studied.'[2] Language can create experience, and political power can control language. For centuries the colonized black man held on to a notion that he was inferior to the white man because the language they both spoke insisted that he was. Of course, he spoke a version of the white man's language in which the qualities of whiteness meant purity and goodness, and the qualities of blackness degradation and devilishness. He experienced his own life in terms of those meanings and images, and believed in them as part of his identity. His language maintained his subservient role in his relationship with the white man, and the definitions of his words vindicated it. Mystification through language is perhaps the subtlest and most insidious technique of domination, and it is still practised on the black man in any country where he speaks a white man's language. A man's language is the strongest factor in his determining of his view of the world and himself. His language translates his world to meaning. His language is his articulated being, is the sense he makes of any aspect of his life and experience. If his language betrays him, his experience is deformed. 'We can be ourselves only in and through our world', says Laing, and when our world speaks division and guilt to us through our language, then we are inevitably divided and guilty.

Between the following two statements, either one capable of being translated into the other, there are two completely different areas of experience, two 'worlds':

It ha' plenty men in Tobago who lime on de street and drink up plenty rum up and down de place. Dey like a whole set of good time and ting.

There are many men in Tobago who meet and talk on the streets, and drink plenty of rum everywhere. They like having good times and enjoying themselves, and going to parties.

In a West Indian island like Tobago, the language tends to divide itself around two standards, both forms of English. There is the local, dialectal, organic English associated with work, folklore and easy communication. It is often a language of growth and spontaneous creativity, the language of identity and belongingness, giving the sounds of a man's essential being in his own world. It is a black man's version of a white man's English, and it has often suited the white man's political power to call it 'Plantation English'. But there is also the other standard set by the colonial administrators and educators, and still very much bound up with the class and status of the West Indian, even as he moves after a new political identity as a part of a 'Third World' nation. This is the Queen's English, the white 'received' standard of written and spoken English, a non-dialectal language, which the aspiring black man, through his education and mystification, imitates. When he takes the white man's language he speaks a language of alienation, he divides himself from the meanings of his words, he begins to talk, like Blackwhite, of black deeds. A lighter-skinned black girl will say of a darker-skinned girl, 'She's as black as an African'. The black man begins to talk of a white man's language in a black man's world. He exists between two ontologies. As Derek Walcott, the St Lucian poet, admits, he is perhaps 'Schizophrenic, wrenched by two styles', and the two styles are two languages, two worlds, two value systems, two opposing political stances, two skins. To change from one language to another is to change life itself: 'To change your language, you much change your life'.[3]

Perhaps in England we have seen a similar problem, but in terms of class rather than colour. Professor Bernstein has shown us how a version of language, be it 'restricted' or 'elaborated', tends to circumscribe the educational chances and lives of children, and how children who move from one of these codes to another 'might be restless in their search for belonging'.[4] They are moving worlds, changing identities. Very often in West Indian society the accepted categories of colour and class have elided; yet white men speaking 'Plantation English' are rare enough. The sociologist Katrin Fitzherbert explains how the double language standard itself brings its divisions in West Indian society and in the individual psyche of the West Indian child:

The syllabus is the crux of the matter, especially as it is in standard English and the children speak a dialect at home. It is the most tangible bringer of double standards into West Indian society. The whole West Indian educational system is borrowed from England, and its prizes via scholarship to university are a wide range of middle-class professions in which even black people can win fame . . . . In fact, a working-class child has very little chance of being a success in the wide society through academic achievements, since it is demanded of him to excel in terms of a language and culture he only partially understands.[5]

The Jamaican psychologist, Godfrey Palmer, remembers his own childhood and education in the context of the violent shift from one language standard to another that the West Indian child is pressured to undergo, both as a young national in his own country, and as an immigrant in England:

Superimposed on his home–school conflict the child has the additional anxiety of being told that he doesn't speak English. Unlike the educated West Indian who knows the difference between standard and Plantation English, the West Indian immigrant cannot always see the difference. He becomes insecure and hurt when it is suggested that he doesn't speak English. His immediate reaction is one of confusion, suspicion and aggression to a statement, which, if true, deprives him of the feeling of belonging that a language confers.

The task involved is not a mere shining and tightening up of a few grammatical points, or the addition of some new words and phrases. It is a whole new language and way of life that is being learned: 'It may be infinitely more difficult for a Jamaican child to unlearn Plantation English, with

its deceptive similarities to standard English, than for a
Greek Cypriot child to grasp the differences between Greek
and standard English.'[6]

The double-standard makes for a confused double-vision.
In the context of this shuffling, the identity of the child is uprooted. He is floundering somewhere between a black and
white world. From feeling relaxed, and possibly unaware of
the extent of his linguistic alienation in his dialectal,
organic English, the new language makes the estrangement
from himself a lot clearer. For the West Indian child as he
moves further into his education, his words become whiter,
but his skin is still as black. And the whiter the words, the
more the mystification process of the language tells him
that he must somehow compensate for his physiological
blackness. He must catch up with the white man. The process becomes more and more insidious, and the idea of
education which implies that a black child, or any child,
speaking a dialectal language, must catch up his elaborated
white fellow, is an idea conceived to tear open the identity
of the child. The point goes a long way beyond the racial:
'The pretext of "catching up" must not be used to push a
man around, to tear him away from himself or from his
privacy, to break and kill him.'[7] Such pressure of alien language and culture on a West Indian child will often persuade
him to throw aside his dialect and sense of linguistic belongingness, be ashamed of his island, his past, his skin, his hair
and his folklore, and frantically and dividedly chase after
the new elaborated standards of the second-hand modernity
of the white man's compensations: the white skin, the
acquisitive life, the divided self.

And
Ban
Ban
Cal-
iban
like to play
pan

at the car-
nival:
pran-
cing up to the lim-
bo silence
down
down
down
so the god won't drown
him
down
down
down
to the is-
land town.[8]

At most West Indian schools, English textbooks are ob-
tained from England. The children study English language
as prescribed by white Englishmen, and read literature
created by white Englishmen. Often they have been taught
English by white Englishmen like myself. The old colonial
preoccupation with the civil service and bureaucratic ad-
ministration has made written received English and O-level
English language the imperative qualification for any job
involving clerical work in those islands still drawing from
the colonial legacy. 'This education is a helluva thing', says
Biswas, and at its spine is the General Certificate of Education (Cambridge and London) English Language examination. Shakespeare, a man much concerned with problems of
the individual's identity ('Who is it that can tell me who I
am?'), gave the situation to his Jacobean audiences seventeen years before the first efforts to colonize Tobago. (In
1628 Charles I gave the island, under Royal Charter, to one
of his nobles, the Earl of Pembroke.) The white, colonial
tutor points out his patronage to his slave, telling him how
many linguistic favours he has done him on his own island
by teaching him a new, sophisticated tongue. He does not
tell him the real truth – that a taskmaster and his slave must
speak the same language to make easy the communication

of services that the slave must perform for his master.
Prospero speaks to Caliban:

> Abhorred slave,
> Which any print of goodness will not take,
> Being capable of all ill! I pitied thee,
> Took pains to make thee speak, taught thee each hour
> One thing or other: when thou didst not, savage,
> Know thine own meaning, but wouldst gabble like
> A thing most brutish, I endow'd thy purposes
> With words that made them known: but thy vile race,
> Though thou didst learn, had in't which good natures
> Could not abide to be with; therefore wast thou
> Deservedly confin'd into this rock,
> Who hadst deserv'd more than a prison.

CALIBAN

> You taught me language: and my profit on't
> Is, I know how to curse; the red plague rid you,
> For learning me your language![9]

Caliban is at least aware of the destructive qualities of the
language which he has learned, and it is important to his
identity that he keeps his rage alive in that language. He
knows, and is angry about his own alienation from the very
language that he speaks. He has recognized the process of
his mystification by his master. When the island reverts
back to Caliban and the colonizer returns home, the language of the old patronage and domination still continues
to rule on in his absence. The de-colonized subject will curse
on in his ex-master's language. That language is still the cur-
rency of communication which buys out the identity of the
black child as soon as he begins to acquire it.

And Shakespeare himself is a part of the whole English
tradition of literature that the West Indian child finds himself immersed in at school. There is perhaps a short play
from Shakespeare put on every year at Speech Day, or
abridged form of the comedies and histories: 'The Shrew
Tamed', 'An Adventure on Gadshill', 'The Pound of Flesh'

– studied from the third form onwards. Then comes O-level, and the English teacher finds himself teaching *Romeo and Juliet* before desks of children with black faces:

ROMEO

O! she doth teach the torches to burn bright.
It seems she hangs upon the cheek of night
Like a rich jewel in an Ethiop's ear;
Beauty too rich for use, for earth too dear!
So shows a snowy dove trooping with crows,
As yonder lady o'er her fellows shows.[10]

Of course, the whole poetic tradition of the white man's language has the roots of its symbolism in the self-vindication and pride of the user. It must be so, if a language is to speak for the people who use it. And if they are white, then the language will naturally vindicate and praise whiteness, and associate it with concepts such as goodness, innocence, chastity, truth. It is the colour of the dove, and the colour of love. And so the natural opposite, the colour of darkness and night, is also the colour of the 'Ethiop' and the crow. And the whiteness and light dominates, shines out from the darkness. The beautiful, virginal white girl, Shakespeare's symbol of hope and rebirth, has her innocence celebrated by her young lover.

FLORIZEL

I take thy hand; this hand,
As soft as dove's down, and as white as it,
Or Ethiopian's tooth, or the fann'd snow
That's bolted by the northern blasts twice o'er.[11]

The blackness is merely the background to the brilliance of the white and its function is to expose and glorify that whiteness. The white man's language speaks this. He makes great poetry out of this. But when the black man speaks it too, he condemns himself and subserves the white man. The dominant images of the language that has been hoisted upon him, and which he continues to adopt, are speaking against him, and gradually eroding his confidence, whether he realizes it or not.

And yet white men sitting in their studies an ocean away in London or Cambridge, will give a tick or an extra mark to an O-level English literature candidate from a Caribbean island who scrambles in from rote a quotation like the one above in his answers. If he has absorbed and remembered the statement against himself and his race, and spills it out over his examination paper, he must get his credit for it. And if he sets down enough quotations like this one inside two and half hours, the chances are that he may pass, and gain more prestige in his island as it pushes for a new identity as a nation. The absurdity of the situation is one liable to constant recurrence while white man's English is continually set as the language and literature norm in Caribbean schools. The same problem will plainly occur in relation to black immigrant children living in England. The old myths and associations of blackness in the English language – like rabid sexuality and diabolism – and the old irrational fears that make the white man close up his heart and mind, will continue as long as the white language and literary traditions are taken literally and seriously enough to make him do so:

IAGO
    Even now, now, very now, an old black ram
    Is tupping your white ewe. Arise, arise!
    Awake your snorting citizens with the bell
    Or else the devil will make a grandsire of you.[12]

The protective response of some children to write 'BLACK IS BEAUTIFUL' across the cover of their English Literature exercise books is plainly the most apt and hopeful comment they can make in such a vicious educational context.

4 English against identity

Prayer of a Black Boy

Lord, I do not want to go into their school,
Please help me that I need not go again,
It's true, they say a little negro ought to go,
So that he might become
Just like the gentlemen of the city,
So that he might become a real gentleman.
But I, I do not want to become
A gentleman of the city, or as they call it
A real gentleman.
I'd rather stroll along the sugar stores . . .

Lord the negroes have had too much work already,
Why should we learn again from foreign books,
About all kinds of things we've never seen?
And then their school is far too sad,
Just as sad as these gentlemen of the city,
These real gentlemen
Who do not even know how to dance by the light of
    the moon,
Who do not even know how to walk on the flesh of
    their feet,
Who do not even know how to tell the tales of their
    fathers
By the light of their nightly fires.
O Lord, I do not want to go into their school again.

Guy Tirolien[1]

In his short story, *Brackley and the Bed*, the Trinidadian novelist Samuel Selvon tells how Brackley, a black Tobagonian, emigrates to England to look for work, and is later pursued there by his old girl friend, Teena. Teena brings the Caribbean with her, and Brackley's English experience soon forces an argument:

'You better go easy with them rations,' he say. 'I not working now and money don't grow on tree here as in Tobago.'

When they was eating Teena say: 'Well you have to get a job right away. You was always a lazy fellar.'

'Keep quiet,' Brackley say, enjoying the meal that Teena cook in real West Indian fashion – the first good meal he ever had in London. 'You don't know nothing.'

'First thing tomorrow morning,' Teena say. 'What time you get up?'

'About nine – ten,' Brackley say vaguely.

'Well is six-o-clock tomorrow morning, bright and early as the cock crow.'

'You don't hear cock crowing in London,' Brackley say.[2]

The story plays out the conflict of some of the opposing factors in the West Indian mind: the opposition between the tropical island life of fruit, fertility and plenitude – the paradisal element – and the English and colonial penumbra of work, money, cities and gloom. As the West Indian child is educated he looks around him, outside his classroom window, and sees lush tropical vegetation, the palms and balisiers, coconut trees, mango trees, bread-fruit, bananas, cocoa. He sees a blue sea, and the sun scorching the red, galvanized roofs of the island's houses. He sees his own world. As he concentrates again on his book he begins to read about another. His mind must be fixed on Europe. In his English texbooks he must read passages and answer questions on, 'We nearly Froze to Death: the story of an Outward Bound Adventure in Scotland', or 'The Coffee-Bar Fashion in London' or 'English Grass Snakes'. He must read about England and white people, in the language of England

and white people as he sits inside his black skin on a small island twenty miles away from South America. His situation is culturally absurd. He is mystified, alienated from his own world, his own island. His situation is a concrete image of Laing's statement, 'We educate our children to lose themselves and become absurd.' The child begins to grow up in another world, an alien one to the world around him. It is as if the closest things to him are irrelevant, his whole organic, immediate life a counterfeit, and the English myths and European dreams the only reality that he must know and recognize. The absurdity has come right down from a colonial, expedient situation. In 1847 the Secretary of State for the Colonies had prescribed an idea of education for the colonized peoples, and the influence of his theme still remains. In a dispatch he wrote of the English language as 'the most important agent of civilization for the coloured population of the Colonies', and the purpose for such education lay in the political relationship between England and her colonies: 'the lesson books of the Colonial schools should also teach the mutual interests of the mother country and her dependencies, the rational basis of their connection and the domestic and social duties of the coloured races'.[3] The duty remains. The child must absorb England through the English language. Consequently her life in Tobago is underwritten by the child, she has been mystified into believing that England and the English world she is educated to share form a better, more sophisticated world than her local, organic, Tobagonian one. English habits *must* be better – her whole education and language have indoctrinated her to believe it. Of Brackley's situation in London, she writes this:

London turns him into a respectable citizen and although
if he had stayed he might have changed, he would not
have become so respectable under Tobago's influence.
London tends to refine many Tobagonians . . .

Thirteen-year-old girl

The statement is an inevitable comment on her education and alienation from her own world. It is as if she must make this statement, in order to vindicate her European education, and speak out against her own identity.

From the extract *Brackley and the Bed*, Brackley seems very ambitious, as can be seen when he leaves Tobago to go to England, which is supposed to be a better place than Tobago.

'Which is supposed to be a better place than Tobago' – she hates to say this, she says it reluctantly, sullenly, but her education has treacherously brought her mind to this point, taken her towards the conclusion for eight years, and thrown her out of her own world. The admission has been a struggle, and it is an admission which she does not want to believe. But to vindicate herself and her lucrative education it is as though she must believe it. When an extended, concentrated secondary school education is as rare as it is in Tobago, she cannot afford to deny the truth of what she learns. But another girl will not agree. Her own world is still too valuable, too strong for her. The world of her education is less valid, and her organic life has kept its primacy. Her identity is more solid, more intact. She is closer to the values of her own island: she rejects foreignness:

In Tobago Teena lived a life where she hadn't to worry about anything. She only had to do her work, and all was well for her. She was accustomed to the lovely beaches and the warm tropical sunshine. The big juicy fruits especially the mangoes whose sweet juice runs down your hand. She was also accustomed to the lovely moonlit nights when she can sit under the tall slender palm trees and relax. She could not enjoy none of this in England. Instead of the lovely moonlit nights and warm tropical sunshine, the nights and days were very cold.

Thirteen-year-old girl

She cannot condemn her real life. She can only flow with it, love it, be it. It has kept its relevance. But with other children the domination of Europe and the alienation process has been made complete.

Indolent Brackley carried his West Indian dialect to
London as if he could not speak better.

Thirteen-year-old girl

V. S. Naipaul has told how his education, in what is considered to be the most desirable of Trinidad schools, forced him to see his own world through the world he read about in English authors like Dickens. It is as if his mind was not allowed to work naturally. It was forced into a foreign, compulsory adaptation. For Dickens's characters:

I have the faces and voices of people I knew and set them
in the buildings and street I knew. . . . Dickens' rain and
drizzle I turned into tropical downpours; the snow and
fog I accepted as conventions for books. . . .[4]

In his novel, *A House for Mr Biswas*, he tells the story of a man who refuses to see his identity in terms of his organic and immediate life and environment. Biswas only sees the world around him as something unreal. In his worst moment it blurs and becomes a void. The realness is far away from him in England: 'There, where Owad had been, was surely where life was to be found.'[5] He never reaches this realness, and his attempts to climb into the illusion that he can through any 'ideal school of journalism' are sad and futile:

Mr Biswas wrote the article on summer; and with the
help of the hints, wrote other articles on spring, winter
and autumn.
   'Autumn is with us again! "Seasons of mists and
mellow fruitfulness", as the celebrated poet John Keats
puts it so well. We have chopped up logs for the winter.
We have gathered in the corn which soon, before a
blazing fire in the depths of winter, we shall enjoy,
roasted or boiled on the cob. . . .'[6]

Biswas becomes absurd. His ideals are dissociated from his life, and his mythology from his environment. He is chasing a distant illusion – the English life – which his education and social standards have projected before him. And the problem becomes even greater for Anand, his son, whose education is more intense. He is crammed with Englishness. Biswas's ideal is an illusion, and it is not surprising that books dealing with real experiences of West Indians in England should have such disenchanted titles as *Journey to an Illusion* or *The Lonely Londoners*. The West Indians' blackness will allow no playing out of the ideal. Many of the present generation of West Indian school children have sensed this, and their level of acceptance of British standards, subject-matter and examinations is much less enthusiastic than either that of Mr Biswas or Anand. A thirteen-year-old girl's comment on *To Sir, With Love* seems to be tinged with far more reality:

The girls and boys tried their best to shock Mr
Braithwaite, a new teacher, but soon he was able to
understand their aggressive behaviour. Then as he was
a black man in England he knew what kind of
experience to expect.

In the Trinidadian play *Moon on a Rainbow Shawl* by Errol John, Ephraim, the young Port of Spain train driver, stares at a Union Jack, and holds his dream of England as the escape from the trapped life in a city slum. The end of the play sees him rushing to the docks to catch his boat. The gradual realization amongst West Indians of the English illusion adds the strongest element of dramatic irony to the play. The absurd and depressing nature of the English reliance, starting from education, is becoming much clearer to West Indian children, and its recognition makes them angry and inquisitive:

... In most secondary schools the books used are
irrelevant to children. Many of the text books, especially
English, are based on aspects of London. The result

of this in many cases is that children fail in GCE, and are, therefore, unemployed by the Government. This examination is also set by Londoners who look at things from their point of view. I think by importing this examination the nation reveals that there are no persons in it capable of setting examinations on West Indian aspects.

Fourteen-year-old boy

An important question that is still left to be answered is whether the GCE, an exam set by English people for English children should be imposed upon our local children without consideration as to its suitability for young people of a young nation.

Fourteen-year-old girl

There is a situation in *Wide Sargasso Sea*, a novel by the Dominican writer Jean Rhys, where the West Indian girl is showing the Englishman her island. He looks through his English eyes at her:

Then she picked another leaf, folded it and brought it to me. 'Taste. This is mountain water.' Looking up smiling, she might have been any pretty English girl and to please her I drank. It was cold, pure and sweet, a beautiful colour against the thick green leaf.

She said, 'After this we go down and up again, then we are there.'

Next time she spoke she said, 'The earth is red here, do you notice?'

'It's red in parts of England too.'

'Oh England, England,' she called back mockingly, and the sound went on and on like a warning I did not choose to hear.[7]

The Englishman brings his standards and his comparisons to an exotic island, and they are good enough for him – they work positively. But they must not be good enough for the children of that island. They will always work negatively for them. And black is the colour of the white man's negative.

A Caribbean climate knows no autumn or spring, in the English sense of the seasons. There is no snow or ice. Walcott speaks of the 'seasonless climate's dry heat or muggy heat or rain'.[8] And yet the illusion of England and the European notion of the seasons and the climate still runs in the mythology of the children as they live in the villages with English names: Scarborough, Plymouth, Richmond and Mount Pleasant. At Christmas they will send each other Christmas cards printed in England, with snow, holly, robins, yule-logs and Victorian gentlemen with stove-pipe hats on them. Ask them to draw a house, and they will often draw a cottage with chimneys. And outside the class-room the sun beats down and scorches the grass, and tourists sprawl on the beaches. Their idea of 'Nature' in poetry is often purely romantic, fictional and European:

A Trip Through Nature

The rivers wide and gushing down
From snowy mountains high
Meandering along the valleys
Where the water birds do cry.

And the ideal of natural womanhood for the child is a white man's ideal with the 'long flowing hair' of Europe:

... To end this trip through Nature
We speak of man supreme
The female with long flowing hair
And man, the god of beauty's dream.

Thirteen-year-old boy

The boy's own blackness is by-passed, and his own beautiful, lush world and environment is substituted by a vague and general world of the imagination, an anaemic Europe. Again, his education, following these dreams, has been self-denying and self-alienating. And he uses a typical old-English-textbook-anthology, conventional poetic rhythm that makes form and content similarly bloodless. He has been turned away from the local and the real, and directed to an empty, joyless, predictable surrogate, the one talked about in his textbooks and school language. If a Tobagonian child is asked to write a poem involving a genuine response to Nature, many times she may come back with something like this: a pretty cameo of idyllic Europe, something perhaps that speaks very generally of the foothills of the Alps:

Spring is Here

Now it is Spring
The trees are blossoming,
The snow is melting from the mountainside
Rivers are flooding the valleys green
Drowning nature's beauty.
Autumn's work has here ceased
The leaves are returning to the branches
And also the beautiful flowers
With fragrance sweet.

This is both a dislocated and fictional vision. The child ignores the real, intense, tropical world around him, to follow after the temperate zones of his European fantasy world. The poem is the obvious consequence of a teaching syllabus which centres around Europe and England, and English cultural traditions. For example, a child will read some extracts from 'In Memoriam', and make these comments:

This poem is about re-birth of Spring after a long winter, as can be seen from the line:
'. . . now fades the last long streak of snow.'
   The last verse is a summary of the others, but this time the poet describes himself as being as lively as the awakening of Spring and the budding and blossoming of his heart, which suggests that he is very, very happy and feels much younger as early Spring flowers when they begin to bloom.

Fourteen-year-old girl

Her remarks are thoughtful and intelligent, and come from a spontaneous response to the poet's mood. Any English teacher would be pleased to read them. But later in the same term, when asked to write a poem about an aspect of her youth, she writes this:

Youth

Oh, how good it is to be young
To feel the green grass on the ground
As you kick your shoes off your feet
To dance helter-skelter on the peat.

To feel the coming of the Spring
To hear the lively sparrows sing
As they build their nests in trees,
Perhaps to get a look at the bees.

So off to the meadows let us go
To see the first Spring flowers on show
And let us dance, make merry and sing,
We're glad to be young – oh, what a good thing.

The influence here belongs to Tennyson: that is clear. It seems likely that she has assimilated Tennyson's English world and English rhythms and versification as definitely the 'poetical' standards which she must follow. Of course, she has put aside the real world around her, considering it unfit and irrelevant matter for poetry and the expression of experience. It is this kind of education, in fact, that works against the expression of experience, pushing the child toward strange and foreign forms and content. So she tries to express, in unfamiliar language, a world she does not know, and will perhaps never know, and so her poetry itself is lifeless and false. Her vibrant enthusiasm for a blooming countryside has been cramped by alien forms. The child loses her real world, and describes another she will never find. The hope lies in the fact that the same girl can write brilliantly, with truth, and feeling, and insight when she writes of her real world, the world she knows. When she writes of the hurricane she experiences (in the first essay on Hurricane Flora, quoted later), she writes for herself and her world, not against them. But here Tennyson and England have become a part of a mockery of education, a process of self-betrayal and alienation, in which the child assumes that the world that gave her life and sensation is beneath poetical expression, and so she must turn to another which is not hers. This is English against Identity.

Those West Indian poets who have been particularly sensitive to the fragility of their identities in face of pressure from the English-type educations, are often forceful in expressing and vindicating the qualities and sensations from their own world in opposition to the temperate, European dream. Here, the Jamaican poet, H. D. Carberry, writes emphatically about Nature and sensation as it belongs to him, as it is wound into his feelings of identity and belongingness to the world around him:

Nature

We have neither summer or winter
Neither autumn nor spring
We have instead the days
When gold sun shines on the lush green canefield
Magnificently.

The days when the rain beats like bullets on the roofs
And there is no sound but the swish of water in the
    gullies,
And trees struggling in the high Jamaica winds . . .[9]

And a fifteen-year-old boy, his childhood home St Lucia, but now a new immigrant at a comprehensive school in East London, with a new notion of 'home' and belongingness, writes about the English seasons as they are, as he knows them, and walks inside them as a part of his world. His poetry gives his impressions of this world without idealism or romantic fiction. The stock images and scenes have also gone with the Tennysonian rhythms and versifications, and

the pictures of a lifeless, predictable world. Now England is
a part of his identity, and not an alien world. His discovery
of the London winter is completely real:

Winters are generally cold and wet and miserable
Like a dog in the rain, or a policeman on his beat,
A time of sitting round your fire and being sad,
A time of watching television and reading and football,
And in the snow, snowballing your friends,
Happy on a sad dark day.

The Forsaken Lover

'My lover is but late today
I wonder what's the matter;
Be it that he no longer cares?
Oh no! he would not cause me tears.

I'll sit and wait, perhaps he's late,
He will not dare to break his date
Those cruel robbers in the square –
Perhaps they've killed my lover there.'

She waited till the evening came
And solemn night approached again,
Till shadows fell softly around
And she could not even see the ground.

She sat there by the window pane
Where she could see both hills and plains,
That if by chance he did come by
She'll be quite sure he did not die.

The sun went down, the stars appeared,
Night's shadow forms were very weird,
Yet there she sat, alone and sad,
To lose him now would make her mad.

She did not sleep a wink that night,
But heard the cock crow for daylight,
Thus many days swept past her there,
She waited for her lover dear.

She mourned with sighing and groaning,
Oh love! Come back to your darling,
O lover dear, why can't you hear?
Sweet mortal, please come near.

Then once she saw a horse galloping
Gliding swiftly over the mountain,
She saw him on the stallion's back
As he rode across the green park,

Hope soared, as he flew towards her,
Her heart reached out to him, her lover,
Then she saw his good companion
Who rode with him on the little stallion.

It was a beautiful maiden
Who had invaded her haven
She didn't want to believe it,
But yet, at least she knew it.

As he approached the little house
His spirit seemed to be aroused,
He hit the horse with all his might
He then shot past her in full flight.

She watched him riding swiftly past,
Her days of love were gone, at last.
He was not dead, but gone for sure,
She had a claim on him no more.

Her heart broke fast and splintered out,
Now she would grieve without any doubt.
Her face grew pale, her limbs grew weak,
Her pretty face was soon tear-streaked.

He married his other lover
And left her alone to suffer,
He had rejected her for sure,
He did not need her any more.

She neither ate, nor drank a sip
To quench the thirst upon her lip
But grief and sorrow was all she knew
As the tree and flowers wildly grew.

Then one day soon the hour had come,
When she, poor maiden, had to be gone,
Her breath was gone, she felt like stones,
While rain and sun did bleach her bones.

Once, later years he did pass by,
And, through the windows he did spy
Yes, she was there, but not his dear.
His love had flesh and she was fair.

Fourteen-year-old girl

I have quoted this poem by a fourteen-year-old Tobagonian
girl in full, because I think it crystallizes much of the previous matter of my arguments. Of course, the rhythm and
metre are often uncertain and uneven and the events of the
last verses somewhat obscure, but the poem's obvious
qualities: the starkness of the theme, the honesty of emotion, the violence of the language and the imagery, and the
sureness with which she sometimes uses the four-line stanza,
make it mature and powerful expression. But the poem, in
its context, is a very strange cultural phenomenon. Apart
from making the odd gesture to modernity ('He will not
dare to break his date'), the black girl in a Caribbean island,
composing at night with the crickets and frogs and pans
sounding outside in the humid, tropical air, writes within
the conventions and structure of the English ballad. She
adopts ballad versification and rhythm, the romance legends
of wild riders and beautiful maidens, the hills and plains of
some fantasy world, the conventional archaisms and
rhetorical exclamations, the stock ballad images ('She felt
like stones') and the heavy, erotic, masculine idea of the
rushing stallion. She even includes a Shakespearian allu-
sion: the 'sweet mortal' is probably due to her study of *A
Midsummer Night's Dream*, and Titania's 'gentle mortal'

wooing of Bottom. Her class was reading the play closely for O-level English Literature during the year she wrote the poem. Her education has stressed to her that this is the way to write poetry: with European themes, environment and myths. The fact that she has been able to produce such a wild and passionate poem inside such alien conventions is an indication of the high merit of her literary skill. Here the fantasy land of the English ballad remains fantasy, remains unreal, and becomes a symbolic land where she can play out her sadness and frustration, a land of the imagination inside her anxiety. There is a very strong sense of the writer's own identification with the forsaken lover herself, and the total sense of loss and decay which she feels, even though she perhaps has in mind a white-skinned maiden. She certainly uses the white image of fatigue and shock when she refers to the 'paleness' of her forsaken lover. The man has found another lover, a 'beautiful maiden', and taunts his old lover by riding past her and callously exhibiting the woman who has replaced her. He is aggressive and pitiless and flaunts his new prize. But the really significant point comes in the last line:

His love had flesh and she was fair.

'She was fair' and the suggestion is obvious, it is written into the child's language and thought, a part of the inevitable and probably unconscious alienation the young girl feels. The new lover is 'fair' and the man has found himself a white lover. The black girl's anxieties and fantasies have suddenly become true. Fair is white, and she is black. Even if the thought was not conscious in her, the language of the self-betrayal and alienation has inevitably made her say it, and once she has said it, she thinks it. It has been said. The white girl is the winner and the black forsaken girl stays in her house and grows old and unloved.

The implication is that the girl, probably without even realizing it, has written herself into a situation of cultural and personal self-denial, and vindication of white people and the white life *merely by using the words that she has always used and she must use.* Merely, in short, by speaking her natural language, made natural by her education. If she doubts that language, she must also begin to doubt her whole way of life bound up inside that language. Her language has made her a loser. It has forsaken her. She has used the language, legends and forms of the white, European world, honestly, passionately, and sometimes brilliantly, but they have finally defeated her and left her loveless and lonely. If she is ever to find her lover again, if she is to abandon her own forsakenness, she must leave Europe and its fantasies, ballads and conventions, its white biases. She must come home:

As I leave Europe
the irritation of its own cries
the silent currents of despair
as I leave Europe
timid in its recovery and boasts
I wish for that egoism which is beautiful
which runs risks
and my ploughing reminds me of a ship's relentless prow.[10]

5 English for identity?

Rain drips
from the trees
in the dawn;
in the morn-
ing bird
calls, green
opens a crack.
Should you

Shatter the door
and walk
in the morning
fully aware

of the future
to come?
There is no
turning back.[1]

In *The Fire Next Time*, James Baldwin described a situation
'where identity is almost impossible to achieve'. The American negro finds himself born into a world which is not his
own, which he can only experience as a white man's world.

The world is white and they are black. White people hold
the power, which means that they are superior to blacks
(intrinsically, that is: God decreed it so), and the world
has innumerable ways of making this difference known
and felt and feared. Long before the negro child perceives
this difference, and longer before he understands it, he
has begun to react to it, he has begun to be controlled by

it. Every effort made by the child's elders to prepare
him for a fate from which they cannot protect him causes
him secretly, in terror, to begin to wait without knowing
that he is doing so, his mysterious and inexorable
punishment.[2]

It may seem surprising to apply this quotation from the
American negro experience to a new nation. Trinidad and
Tobago, with a black prime minister and a predominantly
black government, but the real governor of the culture – the
language – is still in control. The black man still speaks out
his experience in words and symbols belonging to the white
man, no matter how hard he tries to remind himself and
convince himself of the autonomy and dynamism of his
own blackness. As soon as the black child acquires the language, he accepts white forms and sees his experience and his
own skin through a white focus. And, if the child goes to a
secondary school and begins to work towards 'improving'
his English, and drops his dialect and organic speech in
order to speak 'properly', he moves further and further outside his skin and his island. In Tobago, for example, the
'higher' a child moves in his education, the more distant he
becomes from his roots and his past. He begins to shun
them. There follows an unwillingness to accept and consider
his local world, the world that has made him. That world
often becomes too rustic and retrogressive for him, and
sophistication and the modern life seem to lie towards
America and Canada, now the English illusion has largely
been exploded. His acceptance of his past with its associations with slavery become very hard, particularly when he
realizes he is still studying and assimilating in a white man's
tongue. He still finds himself in a situation of linguistic
colonialism, particularly as the secondary education in
Trinidad and Tobago still basically fulfils the old colonial
functions of equipping students for the universities abroad
and the foreign banks and civil service at home.

The new black intellectuals stress the black man's redefinition of himself in the context of his past as well as his

present and future. And if real 'Black Power' is to come, in terms of black people thinking spontaneously as black people in entirely their own psychological context, it can only come organically and naturally if black people adopt a different attitude to the language they speak, a white man's language, which in its use of image, symbol and definition condemns and 'blackens' the name of the black man. The black man must become aware of the extent of his own linguistic alienation. In England, America and the English-speaking ex-colonies, he is assaulted by white norms as soon as he acquires language. As the Boston Schools' Official (a very white man) declared on the subject of English-language teaching to black children: 'We are trying to *break* the speech patterns of these children, trying to get them to speak properly',[3] or trying to get them to speak white by breaking their identities. This is a very violent linguistic process, but as Erikson pointed out, to the white man's notion of history and society the black man's only successful identity has been that of a slave, and it is very often the language that the white man imposes on his black fellows in an area where there is a black immigrant community that is likely to per-petuate such a notion. It is very much like Prospero's trick all over again: give the 'sullen silent peoples' your language, and the debt will stay locked in the consciousness of both sides. The white man calls for gratitude, and the black man curses.

Yet in Trinidad and Tobago, 'correctness' in speech and 'proper' speech are still considered one of the great neces-sities of a child's formal education. There is the standard of the man who reads the BBC news and also the popularity of Choral Speech competitions, a very widely-subscribed sec-tion of the nation's Arts Festivals. This is often judged on the particular group's ability to exaggerate the enunciation of the Queen's English. Vowels are stretched, and con-sonants savoured, mainly to emphasize the 'correctness' of the speech. A lady writing a letter to a Trinidad daily paper made the following statement:

Sir
I have been making public statements of concern for the
language of children – thirteen and under – in the
country. Hence my desire to say publicly that I attended
the finals for 'choral speaking' held at the Queen's Hall
on the afternoon of 11 June. I was very surprised and
overjoyed at the standard of performance I witnessed. . . .

The question I asked myself and others was, why, then,
do our youth speak so bad generally? I fear that the
answer is lack of cooperation by other teachers in the
work for 'better speech' being done by a few.

That 'better speech' is the ability to say the 'set poems'
picked by the adjudicators, all of which are particularly en-
gaging for the glorification of the Queen's English; such as
this one set for children between eleven and fifteen:

Catching Fairies

They're sleeping beneath the roses;
Oh, kiss them before they rise,
And tickle their tiny noses,
And sprinkle the dew on their eyes.

Make haste, make haste;
The fairies are caught
Make haste.[4]

One poem in particular gave the opportunity for an orgy of
vowels that was grasped enthusiastically:

Turtle Soup

Beautiful soup, so rich and green
Waiting for a hot tureen!
Who for such dainties would not stoop?
Soup of the evening, beautiful soup!
Soup of the evening, beautiful soup!
Beau-ootiful soo-oop!
Beau-ootiful soo-oop!
Soo-oop of the e-e-evening
Beautiful, beautiful soup!

And another seemed so foreign to their world as to be completely bewildering:

'O Mary, go and call the cattle home
    And call the cattle home,
    And call the cattle home,
    Across the sands of Dee',
The Western wind was wild and dank with foam,
    And all alone went she.

The one 'local' poem that was used, a poem concerned with the poor people of Trinidad's slums and shanty-towns, seemed to have a lot of meaning for the elder children who spoke it. They found anger and compassion that went a long way beyond flaunting the 'correct' expressions of vowels and consonants in poems about chasing cows around the River Dee:

History Leaves No Memorials to the Poor

History leaves no memorials to the poor
Dulled by their galvanized dungeons
In the step-steepled Laventille
And the Caroni of their sorrows.

Gravid with anguish and the impossible dream
The poor have always rained
Violent weather on each century's scheme
Of temporal precedence.

Violent in their chaste and holy way,
The poor are never proud of ravishment;
A handsome house, an impertinent fence
An intemperate field and the fastnesses
Of the human heart unleavened by love
Are the same presumptuous fortress above
The virgin and the defenceless poor.

The well-remembered image
Locked in the cycle of the crumbled poor
Is the datum of violence
Compiled by every conqueror
Fouling the past and all our tomorrows.

History leaves no memorials to the poor,
The least-loved and the vanquished,
Dulled in their rising steel cities
And their villages of sorrow;
And nowhere are their names engraved
Among the cherished and the saved,
No monuments of stone
Restore to them their perished humanity.

But all their graves lie open
And day by centuries darkening day,
Someone throws in another primordial bone
Or writes a cheque, or looks the other way.

Marguerite Wyke [5]

Once when we were rehearsing a rendition of Walter de la Mare's poem 'The Storm' (a good poem for choral speech, but a very English one), I emphasized to the group that a good effect would be to speak one particular line about the seagulls caught in the storm much louder than the others. 'Say it loud,' I said, 'say it loud', 'I'm black and I'm proud', they all spontaneously shouted back in unison, as if that theme was a lot more real and relevant to their needs than Walter de la Mare's English seagulls.

The tradition of unwillingness to emphasize local themes and issues in education in Trinidad and Tobago has come under sharp criticism in the government's latest draft plan for education in the nation:

Too many persons assume that by making something relevant to the local scene one is, ipso facto, lowering standards. This is one of the attitudes which hamper change and progress, and with which this draft plan is totally unsympathetic.[6]

The government want their education system to have its foundation within itself and not rely on Europe, as its people strive for new identities:

Full national independence and identity will be achieved
and secured only on the basis of an education system
which does not rely on foreign assumptions and
references for its existence and growth.

The new cry is for 'relevance', but the problem really goes
deeper. However relevant the content or subject-matter of
the education is to the people of the ex-British West Indian
islands, the language and its symbols – the form and vessel
of their knowledge – still remain foreign and alienating.
There is plainly a certain kind of English, however, into
which some children can readily and easily relax. In the
story which follows, the sixteen-year-old girl, who speaks
received 'proper' English when she is in school and conduct-
ing her 'formal' education, writes with a natural and
phlegmatic flow, but with a sharp observation and wit, in
her dialectal style, producing a real and close sense of experience. She is writing about her own world in unforced
words which are a part of her own world:

Time, Thelma and Carnival

It was Carnival Tuesday evening about half-past two and
things swinging in town. Bands playing, people jumping
and singing and mas' all about the place: Devils, Red
Indians, Sailors here, Soldiers there, Zulu Warriors from
Africa and in this riot of colour and sound everybody
jumping, jumping to the sound of the sweet pan.

Thelma having a ball. Gone for now was the bitterness
she feel when they order her to come home half-past six,
gone was the hatred she did feel for her grandmother and
her mother that afternoon. She thrilling to the sound of
the sweet pan and showing it like any Tobagonian.

Thelma was in the fourth form of her school; average
height for her age and had enough charm, good looks and
brains to catch the boys. She had a long string of girl
friends too and now she jumping up with them. They
push themselves into the great throng that following 'Our
Boys Steel Orchestra' and they jump from Shaw Park

to Fort Street and then leave the band and return to the
heart of Scarborough to join another one.

On the way down they meet 'Solo Meloharps' going
down. Thelma and her friends at once join in. Suddenly
Thelma remember the time. 'Anybody have a watch?'
she ask her friends, 'Wha is the time?' 'Four o'clock,'
came the answer.

'Good,' thought Thelma to herself. 'Ah have two and
half more hours to go and is a good thing because things
really hot down here.' And with that Thelma let out a
great yell which was lost in all the great noise, and
continued jumping like if she mad.

'Solo Meloharps' stop near the bus-stand to let another
band pass. Thelma and her friends now in the middle of
the band and they frighten because they know when two
bands meet all the drunk men always want to pick a fight
and then if nobody stop them, it always turn out to be a
free-for-all. Then as they half-expect, one of the drunk
men in the band that passing throw a bottle into
'Meloharps' band. Well folks, 'Meloharps' and the
supporters of 'Meloharps' didn't like that at all, so they
start a fight and all the girls and women start running and
screaming and Thelma and her friends get separate. After
some time and with the help of some of the supporters
of both bands, four policemen manage to quell the fight
and carry away the drunk men to sleep it off.

Now Thelma alone. What to do? She ain't have no
idea where her friends are or how to get to them. Besides
it long after four and good pan music playing and
Thelma can't enjoy jumping up by herself.

'You know what it is?' she say to herself. 'I will stand
up in front of Sant's Roti Centre and mih friends bound
to find me.' So Thelma stand up in front of 'Sant's'
alternately looking out for her friends and looking at the
clock in the window. Half-past four. Nobody.
Twenty-five to five. Nobody yet. 'Oh God,' thought
Thelma, 'where mih friends? time flying.' Twenty to five.
Seventeen to five. Thelma watching the clock more often

now. She getting frantic. She toyed with the idea of
jumping-up by herself but immediately she know she
can't do it. Jump-up by herself? Ridiculous, man.
Suppose some fresh man come and hold on to her, what
she going to do? Meanwhile the minute hand creeping
on. Ten to five. Eight minutes to five. Thelma walking
up and down. She can't keep quiet anymore.

'You waiting for somebody, Miss?' inquire a heavy
voice. Thelma look up and see a man with a bottle in his
hand swaying over her. She ain't even bother to answer;
she just run. Soon she reach Scobie's and there were her
friends waiting for her.

'Girl where you were all this time?' her friends ask her,
'if you know how long we stand up here waiting on you.'
'All you telling me,' answer Thelma, 'I was standing up
just down the road by Sant's waiting for all you. Is a
lucky thing that drunk man chase me or else ah woulda
still be waiting down there. Anyhow wha' is the use
arguing, we find each other, leh we go and jump up nuh?'

So Thelma and her friends move out again. It exactly
five o'clock. An hour and a half more to go. Thelma and
her friends have something else on their minds besides
just jumping up. Something to make the jumping up
sweeter.

'Ah wonder where these boys are?' Somebody say,
voicing everybody's thoughts.

'Who woulden want to know?' say somebody else,
again voicing everyone's thoughts.

'Well, who going to miss jumping-up because those
stingy boys ain't here. They mus' be well jumping-up
with some other girls. Leh we enjoy weselves eh,' say
Thelma. This time at the back of her mind, she hope to
see the boys before she go home. The other girls lucky,
they ain't have no old-fashioned mother and grandmother
to tell them to come home half-past six. They could go
home when they want. And again Thelma soul fill with
bitterness. But only for a moment because they had been
threading their way down the road and now they reach

'Symphony Stars' who playing fit to kill. All the bitterness
vanish and she was again full-blooded Tobagonian
Thelma.

The happy girls join the band and then, O sweet
happening! there were the boys that they had been
thinking about.

'Sssst' called the boys.

'Play all you ain't here,' say one of the girls, 'they
bound to come and meet us.'

And she right, because in a minute the boys were with
them. 'Where all you were all this time?' demanded the
boys, mixing with the girls.

'All about the place,' answer the girls carelessly, trying
to hide their excitement.

Then came the sweetest part of jumping-up. The
jumping boys and girls soon divide into couples and go
their own separate way. 'This is living,' thought Thelma
to herself. Time was forgotten and Thelma give herself
up to the magic of Carnival. Soon it begin to grow dark
and the boy at her side hug her closer and Thelma never
feel so happy. Gone were the nagging thoughts of time
and the warning pictures of her grandmother and mother
that had been in her mind all evening.

Thelma and her friend jump down the Milford Road
and back up again. They follow a band up Burnett Hill,
leave it and follow another one down Fort Hill. They
having a grand time. Full darkness descended and the
streetlamps gleamed redly on the faces of the sweating
mass of people. Thelma ain't thinking about aching
arms and feet and worn out shoes.

Sweet pan music playing up Castries Street and of
course Thelma and her friends there. They singing 'Ah
fraid, ah 'fraid, ah 'fraid pussy bite me' . . . as loud as they
could when somebody near Thelma ask, 'What is the
time?'

'Half-past eight,' came the answer.

Thelma world gone flat. Her throat dry. Her feet

moving woodenly. Half-past eight. Oh God, they would skin her alive.

'I going home, yet,' say Thelma to the boy at her side, 'Ah hungry for so.'

The boy look surprise. 'What you mean you "going home"? The night still young.'

'Nah man,' answer Thelma, trying to keep her voice steady. 'I going home, ah hungry too bad.'

'Oh God, you think ah go starve you. Ah go buy something for you to eat.'

'Oh gosh man, doh argue with me, nuh. When I hungry, I real hungry and nothing could fill me up but good food.'

'Allright then,' say the boy, determine for her not to spoil his night, 'Ah go walk you home.'

Thelma see he determine and allow him to walk with her. Thelma set up a fast pace, listening with only half an ear to what her escort was saying. 'Why you walking so fast?' ask the boy. Thelma think fast, 'You ain't feel rain?' she asked. 'It feeling like rain go fall.' This time Thelma frighten for so. The boy ain't saying anything, he just match he pace to the girl own. When they about two hundred feet from the house Thelma say, 'I think you better turn back here. If mih mother see you she going to be vex.' 'More vex than she is now,' added her mind.

'Allright,' say the boy, letting go her hand, 'Goodnight Thelma. See you in school tomorrow.'

Suddenly Thelma can't walk fast anymore. She drag her feet the last hundred yards. Is a different Thelma who creep in by the gate and let herself quietly through the backdoor and into the kitchen. She ate without any appetite, the supper that they leave for her. She eating slow, slow because she want to put off the quarrelling that she sure coming to her. Soon she finish however, and reluctantly she leave the kitchen for the dining room.

As she reach the door, her mother come through it. She begin quietly as always, 'Where you were all this time Thelma?' Thelma ain't answer. She know better than to open her mouth. And then her mother begin to blow all

colour bubbles. 'Look at the time and you now come
home. Half-past six, ah tell you to fin' you' self home here
and now is after nine and you just reach home. What
kinda young woman you going to be? You doh have
respect for nobody.' And so she go on and on for a
whole half-hour. All about how she getting own way
and how she so rude and about past carnivals and about
last year Christmas when she break the nice, new vase. She
finally end with, 'Anyhow, is the las' time you going and
jump-up. Is the last time you even going in town Carnival
day. Now pass and find you' self in you bed before ah come
in there.'

Thelma pass fearfully receiving a box to help her on
her way. She pass her grandmother who just look at her
in a suspicious kind of way and say not a word. She feel
even worse, because although she was feeling hate for her
grandmother that afternoon, she really love her plenty.

Thelma go into the bedroom and change her clothes and
get into bed. She smile to herself in the darkness. The
sting of the slap and the quarrelling already wearing off.
She know her mother say that she wasn't going back in
town another Carnival day, but then she always making
those kind of threats. Besides next Carnival far, far off.
'Carnival tough, tough, tough,' say Thelma to herself, as
she go over all the events of the past evening in her mind.
Then because she so tired, she soon fall into sweet sleep,
sure, sure that the very next Carnival she would be again
in the heat of things, jumping and thrilling to the music
of the sweet pan.

Brenda Scipio

This is real Tobago: the humour, the boisterousness, the
humanity, the flowing with the self. England is forgotten.
Established 'properness' is lifted away, and genuine sensation
and love throb through the writing. Perhaps this is English
for Identity.

The insipid poetry taken from a stereotyped European
fantasy world turns into something dynamic and experien-

tial when the child takes his words from the reality around him. He looks at the setting of the tropical sun, perhaps in the context of the war-scarred history of his island:

The sky's all blood, like a battlefield
With its soldiers all wounded, praying to be healed.

Fourteen-year-old boy

A girl remembers the aftermath of a hurricane:

With a sullen, sonorous sound
The hurricane died down,
Only bits and tins
Left as mark of its sting.

Thirteen-year-old girl

She thinks of some friends leaving her island, perhaps emigrating to England or Canada:

It was their last visit
We were all standing, close together
With our minds based on each other
Saying farewell.

Down the close, darkening road
They made their way
With faces grimly gay
Saying farewell.

They boarded the ship
Without looking back . . .

Another poem speaks of the sea, of its fury and inconstancy, using a strange vision of men salvaging a wrecked ship. The weird empathy the child has with the sea, how it lives and breathes and becomes suddenly murderous, comes through his own unique sensations of his own world, moving through his language and creating a timeless sense of menace:

Ship Wreck

From dawn till dusk they laboured;
But only a few things they had salvaged.
The twisted wreckage of the boat loomed
Silently in front of the shipwreckers.

The shipwreckers were sore and hungry
But there was no time to eat.
They heaved and puffed and laboured
They wondered when they will be released
From this ordeal.

The sea was calm as though unaware
Of what was taking place.
The men heaved a casket of wine which
Slipped and dropped.
As if by chain reaction the sea roared
Its disapproval.

The sea swelled and crashed
And, as if inhaling, took in the men
And vomited their water-logged
Bodies on the golden sand.

Thirteen-year-old boy

English is the linguistic accomplished fact of the ex-British islands of the West Indies, and it has been established as the language of the people, black or otherwise, in islands like Trinidad and Tobago. The previous poems illustrate what a child can very often write unselfconsciously in English, and really express the sounds and experience of his own world. But very often the themes of the mature West Indian writers like Naipaul, Brathwaite, Walcott and Jean Rhys have concerned the search for identity, the sensation of rootlessness and the feeling of isolation. It is as if they have been trapped inside these themes, and have always been nagged to pursue them: Brathwaite's long poem *Rights of Passage* tends to see the problem merely as a purely black one:

Where then is the nigger's
home?

In Paris, Brixton, Kingston,
Rome?

Here?
Or in Heaven?

What crime
his dark

dividing
skin is hiding?

What guilt
now drives him

on?
will exile never

End? [7]

His theme is the uprooted black man, floundering around
the world, looking for a place which will somehow connect
with him:

Ever seen
a man
travel more
seen more
lands
than this poor
land-
less, harbour-
less spade? [8]

It is the 'dark dividing skin' of Brathwaite's black man that
pushes him endlessly forward. Divided from his language
and symbols – the property of a white skin – it can only
harass and torment him. But the feeling of rootlessness cuts
across specific racial identities: Brathwaite's Barbadian
negro, Naipaul's Trinidadian Indian – even the white woman

on the wildest island, seeing her whiteness as the cause of
her isolation ('I wanted to be black. I always wanted to be
black'), makes her own voyage in terms of a young creole
chorus girl in England, moving on from dark, wet city to
city, room to room, her consciousness wavering between her
island and the new country that has always been the country
of her speech and dreams:

Sometimes it was as if I were back there and as if England
were a dream. At other times England was the real thing and
out there was the dream, but I could never fit them together.
  After a while I got used to England and I liked it all
right; I got used to everything except the cold and that
the towns we went to always looked so exactly alike. You
were perpetually moving on to another place which was
perpetually the same.[9]

A great writer – like Naipaul – who writes in a language foreign to his roots and his skin, a language which
is not his, but in fact has to be his because it is the one he
acquired as a child, will inevitably find himself writing
about problems of isolation and identity, alienation and
rootlessness. His identity was somewhere 'out in the void,
beyond the dot of Trinidad',[10] in an area of darkness.
His 'home' was a Caribbean island. His ancestors were
Indian indentured labourers. And he speaks the language
of England. The childhood innocence of sensation and
impression into which the child relaxes before the consciousness of his dividedness, disappears. The mature writer,
it seems, is locked inside his identity problem. A conscious
preoccupation with 'identity' will inevitably become the object of his art. His language, itself a foreign factor, forces
this. A writer must feel good, easy, relaxed in his language,
must be sure that it is his own language, before he can escape
the feeling of unsureness and alienation which a strange
language and culture of unbelonging brings. But Naipaul
shows that great literature can be squeezed out of the taut
tensions generated by the dislocation between language and
identity. His novel *The Mimic Men* is perhaps the culmina-

tion of this tormented feeling. As a vision of the disorder and ruins of a man's own identity, it is stark and horrifying. The 'hero', examining his own devastation, has 'contracted out' of his own and anyone else's identity: 'A man, I suppose, fights only when he hopes, when he has a vision of order, when he feels strongly there is some connection between the earth on which he walks and himself.'[11] But those connections are formed and expressed in and through his own world, that it does not continually betray and humiliate him by the meanings and pressures of its dominant images.

Naipaul said of black writers in America and the West Indies that they tended to trap themselves inside their blackness, and were very often only interested in taking sides and winning acceptance of their racial groups. Blackness 'cannot be the basis of any serious literature', he said. He goes on to emphasize in *The Middle Passage* that the West Indian world has no strong framework of social convention, and can only borrow from the white world: 'the only convention the West Indian knows is his involvement with the white world. This deprives his work of universal appeal.'[12] But it is the wider world in terms of the white world. There is Naipaul himself, or Brathwaite, fulfilling in their own lives the metaphorical search in their novels and poetry: going back to India or Africa, pushing back into their pasts to find roots and meanings that are all transcribed in their art through the white man's tongue. But the West Indian negro's Africanness, Naipaul's Indianness, Jean Rhys's whiteness, all contaminated and afflicted as they are by the Englishman's language, lead the West Indian on more and more to search for his identity in the face of its elusiveness, giving him a continuous metaphor for his journey, taking him further into the most universal of problems.

In the context of this massive preoccupation with identity in West Indian writing, the arguments against the present structure and material of English education in the West Indies are obvious: the irrelevance of much of the subject-matter, the bad examination system which gives power of pass and fail to obscure examiners in England who may know nothing of the West Indian ethos, and the lack of confidence in local themes. If one considers these disadvantages inside the alienating force of the language that teacher and child speak, there is plainly much that needs changing. The main problem seems to be: how do you make black children aware of the dangers of the language which they speak, without stunting their usage of its communicative, creative and enduring qualities? My main contention is that such a child *must grow up on English as spoken by his own people inside the society which is to be his*, rather than English as spoken by Englishmen. He already is inside a great literary tradition, and even now there is enough substantial West Indian literature to furnish both a profound and varied English school curriculum at all ages and levels. If he is to read English literature by English authors, he should see it in the context of his own West Indian literary tradition and not vice versa. He should not be sold the English tradition before he knows and has explored his own. If he is to study Shakespeare, it should be in the context of his own world and his own writers' use of English. He should not be given the odd token gesture of Caribbean literature in the surrounding context of Shakespeare, Wordsworth and Jane Austen.

His education must place him in a tradition of his own, and give him the secure sense of cultural belongingness that every person needs as a basis to think and act. His knowledge of himself and others must come inside a feeling of sharing a common literary identity inside his particular world and people. Education inside any other foreign culture means dependence and subjection to that culture. It is the way back to colonialism and absolute reliance on alien standards controlled by foreign people. And to the black man, white standards of language and culture are essentially oppressive standards which maim and destroy his belief in himself. George Jackson (*Soledad Brother*, p. 30) looked back to his own school life and concluded:

I know now that the most damaging thing a people in a
colonial situation can do is to allow their children to
attend any education facility organized by the dominant
enemy culture.

The same kind of awareness is happening at the classroom
level in Trinidad and Tobago. In the *New Beginning*, the
newspaper of the Trinidad and Tobago Coordinating Committee, a black student wrote (2 April 1971):

Another fact which the system seems to overlook is that
the bulk of students are black and the education which
we receive is white. The result is a black student with a
white mind. With his white mind the black student
completely forgets his colour and enters white society. . . .

   The whole cause for the shortcomings in our
education system is the GCE. We allow those 'beloved'
Englishmen to set our standard of Education for us. We
allow them to dictate what we must and we must not learn,
when it would be in their interest to keep us ignorant.

   . . . It is quite clear that Mr Cambridge and Mr Oxford
cannot begin to know a thing about our society. . . .

In Trinidad and Tobago the General Certificate of Education examination, prescribed and marked in England, holds
even more significance than it does in England. Any clerical
work or civil service post requires O-level English language
(the ability to communicate like an articulate white man),
and there is often a hostile desperation for a West Indian
child to pass the examination that makes him turn to private
tuition and frantically write after Wolsey Hall correspon-
dence courses. In a country where so many young people
are unemployed and a job in the Government Service or
Banking seems to represent the change from labourer to
civilized man, O-level English language becomes like a
guiding star. It exerts a depressingly huge influence as a
token of acceptance into the white man's standard of expression and culture. As such it becomes an important
weapon of white domination and black estrangement. The
academic future of the West Indian is still decided in Oxford

and Cambridge. Without his A-levels he cannot gain admission even to his own Caribbean university. The colonial structure still controls any educational progress the West Indian tries to make.

This situation becomes even more absurd when the power and many-sidedness of so much Caribbean culture is examined. There is no need to argue the merits of Caribbean literature. Is there a better novelist in England than Naipaul? Are there better poets than Brathwaite or Walcott? These writers should be read and studied closely in English schools as well as in the Caribbean: English people, black and white, have so much to learn from them. And there is the whole tradition of Black American literature and African literature, with books about growing up black in a white man's world, the awakening consciousness of the black child in that world: Richard Wright's *Black Boy* or Camara Laye's *The African Child.**

But it is the GCE structure which sets the syllabus and cultural direction, and as long as it continues to exist in the Caribbean, that direction will always be towards England. Everything that he reads tells the child that his educated eyes must stare longingly towards England. His own island, his education tells him, is not a place for the intellectual. Education means exile, even when you sit in the Caribbean classroom. Why set *The Long and the Short and the Tall* for O-level, a very 'English' play reliant on much of its dramatic power on the strong interplay of regional British dialects, when there is an excellent play in *Moon on a Rainbow Shawl* set in Port of Spain, and very skilful in its use of Trinidad themes, dialects and speech rhythms? Why teach *Jane Eyre* for O-level when there is a very fine Caribbean sequel in *Wide Sargasso Sea*? Why study novels about problems in English society when sharp social commentary on West Indian themes can be found in books like Mittel-

*The 'novel of childhood' is a particular strength of Caribbean literature. Michael Anthony's *The Year in San Fernando* and George Lamming's *In the Castle of My Skin* are especially fitting for school-children to study. They would give the world of the child back to the child.

holzer's *A Morning at the Office*, or Patterson's *The Children of Sisyphus*? Why study Mark Twain, Jules Verne, John Masefield or Jack London in the first and second years when there are novels for younger readers like Namba Roy's *Black Albino* or Andrew Salkey's *Hurricane*? And there is the work of Wilson Harris, Lamming, Hearne, Selvon and Lovelace. Any arguments for continuing with a dominantly 'English' English would seem very slight with such an impressive Caribbean output. And in his excellent anthology of West Indian writers for school children in the Caribbean, Kenneth Ramchand has this to say about the teaching of literature in Caribbean schools:

But there is also a positive indifference to literature on the grounds that it is neither enjoyable nor useful. It is seen as the worst of school subjects, something which has to be learnt, but which, after all the trouble, has no connection with one's own life and interests, a bookish subject which is useless as soon as one leaves school. . . .

These attitudes originate and are consolidated in the schools. For the student, literature has generally meant English Literature, which is set in a foreign country, which contains English characters and English situations and which, in many ways, is rooted in English life and manners. It is possible to read and enjoy this literature, but the younger reader may find it difficult to see beyond what he takes to be its Englishness.

The local details in geography and culture are often outside his experience, and sometimes difficult to imagine: whereas these details usually function in an unobtrusive way for the English reader, the West Indian student is constantly distracted by their foreignness and novelty. . . .

The foreignness of English literature operates to the disadvantage of literature in another way. Some of the situations which arise in English fiction are not immediately relevant to the West Indian student or to the society of which he has direct experience. The student therefore rarely becomes involved, and what is probably worse, he begins to build up the attitude that literature has very little connection with life and society.[13]

His remarks are easily supported by the apathy and bored faces of the Tobagonian children reading *Short Plays from Shakespeare*, or *A Journey to the Centre of the Earth*, and the very different interest and enthusiasm radiated for his own anthology, particularly for stories like *Kanaima*, by Wilson Harris, with its setting amongst the Amerindians in the Guyanese jungles, or *Brackley and the Bed*, with the strong humour of the West Indian's London exile.

> they go to school to the head-
> master's cries,
>
> read a black-
> board of words, angles
>
> lies;
> they fall
>
> over their examinations.
> It is a fence that surrounds them.[14]

It is plain that mere relevance, or a shift in focus from the London streets to the Caribbean palm trees, is not enough. The problem goes beneath the locale and themes in the literature of the language itself. The damage is done there. The English teacher in the Caribbean must be assiduous in explaining to his students, as their capacities for criticism develop, the dangers of the language which they speak. A black child should never be expected to unquestionably accept the symbolic meanings of black and white in the English language based as they are on the vindication of whiteness and the degradation of blackness. Such a language speaks against him and lies about his beauty, his hopes and his realness. He should be introduced to a consideration of the way in which the white man uses these symbols, and how he may possibly find himself using them. He must not accept the white man's lies against him, lying as they do in the very basis of the symbolism of the language, and neither must he unwittingly lie and malign himself. If English has become his language, then he must speak it, but it must not

destroy him or drive him from himself. Such expression and
sophisticated language like the previous quotations from
Shakespeare should be critically examined and discussed, so
that the child begins to take on awareness and knowledge,
not dividedness and guilt. Why should black have these
meanings? What does the adoption of the white man's language mean in his life? How far does it compel him to strike
an apologetic tone for his blackness:

MOROCCO
  Mislike me not for my complexion,
  The shadow'd livery of the burnish'd sun,
  To whom I am a neighbour, and near bred.[15]

He will begin to see that there may be strong and extreme
differences between the way in which the white world sees
him and speaks about him, and the way in which he will
choose to see himself. When he has discovered this he will
know that it is his own view and the view of his own people
that matter in the passage of his life, and he will begin to
control a language and a world capable of enclosing and
defeating him. He will begin to see that there are other times
when black means beautiful and white is the colour of snow
and coldness and skin as 'white as leprosy'.[16]

A teacher read,
He read on and on
About colour,
I just glared
The period ended
He demanded to know what I was
    glaring at,
I told him
I was admiring his arctic colour.
He glared more,
And shouted me down to the head.
The head quietly asked what happened.
I told him everything, the teacher's
    part and mine.

He replied,
Saying it was his job
And that I had a point too.
He said again he'll just give me one.
I told him there was small justice,
For saying that I got two.

Fourteen-year-old boy

And when it is also the insidious whiteness of the whale:

... yet for all the accumulated associations, with whatever
is sweet, and honourable, and sublime, there yet lurks
an elusive something in the innermost idea of this hue,
which strikes more of panic to the soul than that redness
which affrights in blood.

   This elusive quality it is, which causes the thought of
whiteness, when divorced from more kindly associations,
and coupled with any object terrible in itself, to heighten
that terror to the furthest bounds. ...

Herman Melville, *Moby Dick*

He will begin to find new symbols which speak of him, not
against him. He will make changes in his language. He will
find his own 'English' which is not English, and break the
white confines around his words and mind. He will write in
the way most 'proper' to him – the way which tells of his
own world and himself.

   But this can only be achieved if the shift of standards,
criteria and focus from London to the Caribbean is managed. While London still rules West Indian education by her
examinations, textbooks and literary standards, any hopeful
notion of the autonomous political or cultural power of
blackness in Caribbean communities remains futile and
stillborn.

6 Drama and identity

To educate a man to be ACTIONAL, preserving in all his relations his respect for the basic values that constitute a human world, is the prime task of him who, having taken thought, prepares to act.[1].

No, we do not want to catch up with anyone. What we want to do is to go forward all the time, night and day, in the company of man, in the company of all men.[2]

'Identity' itself, the feeling of belongingness, is the most necessary feeling that any individual needs in any society, but when a new nation is asserting her own newly-wrought independence as a new political entity, the notion of 'Identity' amongst its young people will have a special importance. These are the people who will be responsible for maintaining that hard-won concept of national identity, and it seems necessary that their English education, through essays, discussion and debates, should suggest to them exactly what that means. Not in any doctrinaire approach, but merely by stimulating an awareness of their own nation's aims and means of government in the context of world organizations and movements. It seems absurd in itself that any school 'subject' concerned with Caribbean life, culture and Identity should still be called 'English'. Perhaps the subject would carry less weight of alienation if the name itself was changed.

But the idea of political awareness as a part of their 'literary' education is particularly important for ex-colonial peoples who have lived for long periods with subjection, and have often come to accept it in the same way that they have accepted and adopted the white man's language. The awakening awareness of the linguistic colonization which still oppresses them has a strong alienating effect which could possibly create either a very aggressive attitude to the white world and its forms and cause them to curse like Caliban in the white man's language, or it could induce a high level of apathy and cynicism which would have a deadening effect on their consciousnesses both as individuals and nationals. There is still the feeling amongst many black children in the islands that if they had the power and choice, they would rather be white. This is the consequence of the symbols they have always used in their language which say, in short, that it is better to be white. So then the black child will be on the defensive to protect his skin, in the face of the accusations made about it by the language which he and the white English world both speak: 'It's not my fault I'm black,' he says, 'and anyway, what's wrong with being black?' These undercurrents of self-defensiveness very often show themselves when a black child considers that either he or his race has been wronged. And then even by protecting himself, the white words which he uses will accuse him again, and apologize again for his blackness. A fourteen-year-old Tobagonian girl wrote this in an essay on student militancy:

In Sir George Williams University in Canada, many negroes are being repeatedly failed in their examinations. This should not be. Man likes to own and be master, he likes to be powerful and important. These being man's chief qualities, if he knew that white would be the ruling colour, and he was responsible for the colour of his skin, he would surely have it changed to white. But he is not to be blamed for being black, then why should such unjust penalties be imposed on him?

From this tone of passivity, forced upon her by the power of the white bias of the language she has to use when referring to 'colour' differences, she changes to something more positive:

A professor had deliberately failed a Negro student because of his colour, and passed an English student on presenting a duplicate of the Negro's work.

Such acts of injustice only raise the colour barrier higher. They impose upon the negro population great hatred for the white population. No man would sit back and be cheated without fighting for his rights.

The economic plight of the West Indian is stressed. His lack of money for a university education, just like his language, throws him back on the favours of white people and compromises his skin, his dignity and his independence. And the girl has to retreat again when she comments on the militant action of mistreated West Indian students at a Canadian university. The language plight and the economic plight elide. Both areas are dominated by whiteness, and the black child steps down:

The negroes exhibited their bad manners and long-restrained rage by this vicious action. It was one of the worst possible things they could have done and it would have some very bad effects on the younger people who are hoping to enter a university.

Now that these misfortunes have arisen, there would be little or no chances of any negro entering the Canadian university in future. Negroes would no longer be trusted or accepted by the Canadian Government. The Canadian Government would no longer give negroes scholarships to their universities.

The girl's concluding analysis of the world problem between black and white suggests the nature of the struggle almost in the way that Fanon saw it: the white man consolidates and continues the politics of domination because of his fear of the black 'take-over', whereas the black man of the 'third world' tries to improve his conditions in his own cultural context, away from the domination of Europe, and asserts his own culture in the face of inevitable comparisons:

It is more likely than not, the white man is deliberately suppressing the black man for his own selfish reasons. He is afraid of losing his power and wealth to the black man, while the black man is desperately struggling to improve his present conditions.

If every one explored the main objects of these turbulent uprisings they would find no other reason than racial discrimination as the cause. If only racialism can be dispelled from these societies, these problems would be overcome. This is the only alternative, since black and white men would always exist.

'Since black and white men would always exist.' But how to make them coexist without the white domination of the black, particularly in an education situation where the black man speaks the language and unwittingly asserts the symbols of the white world? The poetical answer seemed to be to make the world, white and black and yellow, come to Tobago, so it became the political centre of the world, the stage of world affairs, as it must be for the children who are going to live there and find their identity with the island. If it is a fiction that Tobago is the centre of the world, is it not a fiction that Tobago is the centre of the world for Tobagonians. For Tobagonians, the world must unashamedly be seen in the context of Tobago, from the standpoint of Tobago. So the world came to Tobago in the form of mock 'United Nations General Assemblies', organized to provide a theatrical and humorous experience, as well as a politically earnest one. For a few afternoons Tobago became the world's political platform and stage.

The prime mover in the 'assembly' became Trinidad and Tobago. The Trinidad and Tobago delegates, assuming the garb and deaf-aid of the Prime Minister, Dr Eric Williams, initiated the 'Draft Resolution', and was the first speaker to vindicate it. The resolutions were drawn up with a great deal of seriousness, normally at the time when the issue involved (for example Rhodesia, Anguilla) was at some climax of world affairs. Here is a part of the resolution used for the 'assembly' on the Rhodesia problem:

Draft Resolution moved by Trinidad and Tobago

Realizing that the Universal Declaration of Human Rights is a common standard of achievement for all peoples and nations.

Having considered the report on the special committee on the policies of Apartheid of the Government of Rhodesia.

Convinced that the situation in Rhodesia and South Africa continues to pose a threat to International peace and security.

Considering it essential to promote a closer and greater coordination of international efforts to eliminate Apartheid and racial discrimination in Rhodesia,

The Government of Trinidad and Tobago

1. Reiterates the condemnation of the policies of Apartheid practised by Rhodesia as a crime against humanity.
2. Reaffirms the recognition of the legitimacy of the struggle of the people of Rhodesia for human rights and fundamental freedoms for all of the people of South Africa irrespective of race, colour or creed.
3. Strongly reiterates its conviction that the situation in Rhodesia constitutes a threat to international peace and security, that action under chapter 7 of the Charter of the United Nations. . . .

The children made their contributions with great conviction, each one representing a specific nation involved. They had examined the policies of the particular nations they represented, and now assumed the normal attitudes of their nation to such a resolution in their speeches. There was some unlikely and sharp humour: bomb scares, assassination attempts, Arab–Israeli bombast and outside demonstrations, and the boy who played the South African delegate appeared with his face blanked out with flour. But it was also very much of the politics of sympathy and experience:

Firstly, the policy of Apartheid needs condemnation because it entails separation and 'separation' is an ugly word. . . . Let me give you some insight as to the gross discrimination practised in Southern Rhodesia. I was flying to Zambia, but in order to break the long journey, my plane stopped at an airport in Salisbury, and Mr President, I was denied lunch because I was the sole negro. It was a long, a very long trip, tired and hungry I was, but incredibly enough, I did not eat. On this trip, I also learnt that negroes are not allowed to try on or touch material in stores – probably it is thought that when the negro comes into contact with the cloth, a disease will be passed from the negro to the cloth. Negroes are forbidden to enter bars and drink rum at a place called Lusaka in Northern Rhodesia. A negro to whom I was speaking on my last visit to Rhodesia announced :

'We don't want permission to enter the white man's bars, what we want is proper education, and to have a say in affairs of government – the white man still thinks of us as children.'

There it is, Mr President, the Rhodesian European still thinks of the average negro in terms of the African negro imported to the West Indies about 400 years ago!

Fifteen-year-old girl

The black child in the Caribbean island becomes the African again, goes back to her roots and, in her imagination, begins to know and feel Africa again, and the trials of her fellows there. Her identity leaves Europe even further behind, and moves towards both a confirmation of itself, and a fusion with the other peoples of the third world.

When I was hungry, you fed me books, Daniel's dungeons now I am thirsty, you would stone me with syllables.

We seek we seek
but find no one to speak

the words to save us.[3]

Perhaps Brathwaite's words point to the conscious or unconscious levels of bitterness that a black West Indian child may
have towards the words he is compelled to speak at his
school. They are words which do not 'save' the speaker, but
condemn him against himself. It seemed imperative to try
to get the children writing and acting from their own experience, and not a borrowed, colonized one, in the language
and style of movement which gave them most ease. But in
Tobago there was often a sense amongst the children that
they must turn aside from their own world, to shun things
local, and stretch after the world which seemed to form the
approved subject-matter for the 'proper' language stressed
in their schools. Many of them were the sons and daughters
of middle-class civil servants and shopkeepers – themselves
very much intimidated by, and sucked towards what
Naipaul calls a dream of 'modernity' in *The Middle Passage*,
the reaching after the modern' world in Europe and
America with their seductive domestic technology and
fashions. The tradition at school had always been to act out
a short play from Shakespeare at most speech days, together
with other contributions by the choir and dance group. The
Shakespeare play had given them the chance of dressing up
in exotic foreign costume (itself a very important part of the
ritual of the yearly Carnival), to make themselves up and to
speak out good and proper super-enunciated language, and
generally display their level of acceptance and assimilation
of the white man's English and theatrical deportment. The
suggestion that perhaps we should try to act a play with a
more relevant and 'local' theme was greeted with horror by
some girls, who immediately dissociated themselves from
any such production. A play on a local theme set in a fishing
village at the time of Hurricane Flora, which devastated the
island in 1963, seemed to some of the girls only to be about
'a lot of old fishermen', and was hardly the elevated subject
for a speech-day drama. The theme seemed too local and
rustic for them. It was as if their education was designed to
enable them to escape from these things, and to concentrate

the educational focus on their own island and world was an unnecessary and retrograde step.

The idea behind such a play came after the children had written in class essays some earnest and eloquent accounts of the hurricane as they had experienced and remembered it. We were also reading some excerpts from Andrew Salkey's novel *Hurricane* at the time in class. Salkey's novel is set in Jamaica and is very successful in expressing the real, instinctive responses of a young boy towards the sudden and violent upheaval of normal life. The children were asked to write an essay concerning an aspect of danger and violence that they would remember in their lives. Many of them responded by describing their own experience of Hurricane Flora, plainly a critical event in their lives when their childhood life underwent a sudden and violent disruption in the context of suffering, perplexity and death, all dominating the atmosphere of tragedy:

The sun rose in a very clear sky. I awoke with a feeling that something very unusual was going to happen. I think it was because of the dream I got the night before.

At nine-o-clock, grey dismal clouds started to form in the sky and I had not left for school as I could get no transport. The rain began to fall and I gave up all hopes of getting a vehicle. I was just about to go home, when a car stopped and offered to take me to my school, which was twenty miles from where I lived.

That morning I reached school one hour late, much to the disapproval of myself and my teacher who is a lady who likes strict discipline.

At eleven-o-clock the rain was still pouring heavily. The seas were behaving as if they had a monster. The waves crashed on the beaches. The little boats that were in the sea started dashing about and many were destroyed by the thundering waves.

Church bells started ringing, the sirens started screeching, and it was then that I realized that we were about to experience our first hurricane in decades. The children were very panicky when they heard the news. Many cars came to take home their usual passengers.

As I was living very far from school, I had to wait until the evening when my father came to take me home. Many of the children had left by twelve-o-clock, and very soon there were only nine children (who like me were living far), who were left in the school.

The school-house was a very old building. Two little girls were playing hide-and-seek, unaware of what was going on. One of them went to hide below a bench near a window. It so happened that as soon as she was about to come out of her hiding place, the partition by the wall caved in and pinned the little girl to the floor. Her friend saw her fall, but being a little girl, she stood watching.

I was upstairs with the other girls and I noticed that I was not hearing the little girl's laughter. We descended the stairs and as we touched the landing, the girl who was watching ran to me and started maundering and pointing frantically towards the caved-in partition. After a minute she fainted in my arms. The other girls ran over to the partition and freed the girl. She opened her eyes, watched us, and then shut her eyes as though she had fainted. By that time I was really frightened.

An hour later my father came for me and he took her to the hospital, where she died on arrival.

I was very sorry and still frightened. It seemed as though fate was against me. On our way up, as my father was passing a place by the name of 'Bad Rock', many big boulders starting rolling down, forming an avalanche blocking our path. It was two hours before we could continue our journey.

We reached home without further incident, and I was very glad when my mother gave me a hot bath, a cup of coffee and put me to bed as though I were a baby. I was very glad to go to bed to shut out all those horrific thoughts.

Thirteen-year-old girl

I was at home when I turned on the radio, to hear the news. The news I got was very shocking, it was a hurricane warning. We were told to buy special amounts of food and other necessities. The news was broadcast at two p.m. and two hours later it started.

By now everyone was at home. Shops, stores and other business places were closed, and everyone waited this dreadful happening.

The seas started making a horrible noise, while the waves rolled angrily and devouringly. I looked out of the window and saw the winds tossing the trees here and there with violent force. The roofs of the houses were lifted and thrown into the yards of other houses.

People were crying and praying because more and more the water was rushing in and out of their homes, to get refuge with others that had not as yet been destroyed.

To keep the coldness from us we lit a huge fire and sat around it, eating some delicious hot porridge. While eating, we heard a loud crashing noise, and when we looked, we saw that a coconut tree had fallen onto the roof of our house, causing the wind and rain to come in more freely and desperately.

About half-past five the wind grew so much stronger that we began to tremble and murmur with fright and longing.

At six p.m. the hurricane ended abruptly and everyone was glad. We slept very soundly through the night, and in the morning the sun was shining brightly, the birds were singing sweetly and everything was normal and usual.

After clearing up, we prayed, that nothing like that will ever happen to us again.

Thirteen-year-old girl

On September the thirtieth 1963, I had the most memorable experience of my life. This is a live story of how it all happened.

On the beautiful morning of September the thirtieth, I, because of illness (influenza), stayed away from school.

The morning was bright and sunny, but slightly windy.
My three brothers had actually gone to school, so
Vernon, a cousin of mine, my younger sister Linda, my
mother and I were at home.

All of a sudden the wind began increasing and so I
began to question my mother, 'Mammy, did storm ever
come in Tobago?' I asked. 'Yesson, once when you was a
little baby,' she said. 'But Mammy, look like a storm, look
how the banana trees falling down,' I said. 'Boy don't
talk stupidness, eh.' But the wind continued increasing.
Then I heard Mammy's voice saying 'Boy it look as
though yuh talking truth, yes. We better go upstairs.'

By the time we were upstairs and finished closing the
windows, there was a resounding crash. The avocado
tree, laden with beautiful fruit had fallen about two
yards from the northern side of the house.

Coconut trees all around the house kept falling, some
of their heads twisted as though the mighty hand of some
unseen giant kept wringing them. Limbs of the cedar and
bayleaf tree were being hurled like arrows through the
air. There was a deathly calm.

At about one p.m. the first part of the hurricane had
passed, and the principal of the elementary school urged
all students to try to get home before the second half
struck. Fortunately my elder brother reached home in
time.

Vernon and I, at the interval of the hurricane, went out
to the back yard to gather coconuts (water nuts) for
drinking purposes when the second half came.

The second half of the hurricane came from the
south-east just opposite to the first part; it came with a
terrific force and a spinning motion, at about 120 m.p.h.
The noise the wind made was like that of a jet plane
whistling through the air.

In front of our house there are two large cedars and a
bayleaf tree. Had it not been for these trees our house
would have been destroyed. Like a boy raising the roof of
his toy house, half of the roof of the shop which is also in

front of the house came flying through the air and smashed with unbelievable force against the cedars and bayleaf tree. It wrapped neatly around the trees like the hand of a man around match sticks.

The wind continued blowing with sheets of rain splashing against the house. Just to say how strong the wind was, Vernon and I went downstairs. When we opened the door both of us together could not close it back because of the force of the wind.

The wind decreased slowly after its destroying work was finished.

Nine people died, four-fifths of the houses were either destroyed completely or damaged. At the end of the hurricane, the island looked as though bombs had been dropped ten feet apart all over the island.

Thirteen-year-old boy

The structures of these essays, following the gradual and portentous growth and explosion of the hurricane and the calm and aftermath of its destruction, are dramatic and tragic in themselves. There is a natural conflict and climax in the event itself, and also in the children's response to it that seemed ideal for theatrical experience. If they could act out a situation caused by the hurricane, and transpose their stage into their island, it seemed that such a play would reflect very much their own world, and their knowledge of themselves up against the most violent upheaval of their lives. It would be an organic extension of their identities. The people in Trinidad and Tobago have a very strong dramatic tradition which has kept its popularity in the Carnival and 'Old Mas', but somewhere drama at this school had distanced itself from their lives and gone to Shakespeare. It had become a part of the inhibited, academic world of the GCE syllabus and 'proper' English language and literature. Now it seemed very necessary to bring it home again, in a way that caused it to reflect real life and experience.

Using the structure, and much of the material of the essays that the children had written, I conceived the framework of a short play about the hurricane. I suggested themes and guide-lines for individual speeches, hoping that the players would improvise themselves, and use their own speech rhythms and structures to go in their own directions and forge out their own dialogue from the guidelines I had given. I was a foreign, white teacher, paid by the government to train the children towards their GCE certificates and I was writing these speeches in received English. So to make their dramatic experience anything like authentic, the children would have to be both emotionally and verbally creative, and remember and imagine vividly the heavy experiences of six years earlier. Some of the cast hardly veered from the ideas and themes I had suggested in the guide-speeches, only saying them in a semi-dialectal way, and I wondered if I had imposed too much of a structure on them. But the actor playing the main character – Hawkins – and also those playing Mrs Daws and the fisherman Carrington, only used the suggestions in the guidelines for bases of high flights of improvisation in the language they knew best. Some lines were already fixed – such as those spoken by the 'Spirit of the Hurricane', a morality play figure who speaks like a stranger in 'proper' received English – and a few stylized lines spoken while the hurricane is blowing in its fury, but new lines and movements were often bursting out at all moments in the more realistic sections of the dialogue. The character of 'Hawkins' came to life very much because of the huge creative charge given to the part by its actor. He lurched, sprawled, belched, poured buckets of water over himself, and really lived the part, making it grow in his own style. Later on in the year when he was reading the part of Bottom in the Shakespeare text we were studying for O-level English literature, he read using many of the traits he had developed as Hawkins. He began to see Shakespeare inside the context of his own world.

We tried to suggest the elemental fury of the hurricane by using the natural sounds that were available to us, in a discordant combination which reminded many of the audience of the real cacophonous experience. The frantic banging of three African drums out of time with one another combined with the crashing of galvanized iron sheets beaten by pieces of lead pipe accompanied the loud and terrified shouts and screams of human voices. This was synchronized with the stylized cruel and violent movements of figures at the front of the stage, struggling with the monstrous wind. At the back of the stage, various pieces of debris – palm branches, coconut husks, pieces of wood, pipe, tree-trunks – were hurled from wing to wing. And behind the action and sound the lighting went on and off in intermittent and uneven flashes, lighting up the stage, then plunging it again into darkness. The total effect became a multi-media experience into which the children flung themselves with a combination of remembered fright and passion, and dramatic discipline. The sound stopped and started, leaving brief periods of uneasy silence in which the characters said their stylized lines, often punctuated by short, violent bursts on the African drums and flashes of coloured lights. The use of folk-songs at the beginning and end of the play suggested the same continuity of life before and after the disaster that the children had expressed in their own accounts of the hurricane. The play was always a living and growing thing, and by the time they had acted it publicly several times – each time adding fresh embellishments – and won the nation's Junior Arts Festival with it, it was really the children's play, a reconstruction of their own experience.

We had tried to show the island as a real place: real in the sense of being a place of real men who eat and fish and drink and sleep and suffer. To make the stage a world for Tobago, certainly, but also as part of a greater and bigger world, giving it the poetry of reality, of children at ease with their own language, on their stage, their island, their world:

It is not enough
to pray to Barclays bankers on the telephone
to Jesus Christ by short wave radio
to the United States marines by rattling your hip
bones.

I
must be given words to shape my name
to the syllables of trees

I
must be given words to refashion futures
like a healer's hand

I must be given words so that the bees
in my blood's buzzing brain of memory

will make flowers, will make flocks of birds,
will make sky, will make heaven,
the heaven open to the thunder-stone and the volcano
    and the unfolding land.

It is not
It is not
it is not enough
to be pause, to be hole
to be void, to be silent
to be semicolon, to be semicolony;

fling me the stone
that will confound the void
find me the rage
and I will raze the colony
fill me with words
and I will blind your God.[4]

I Thought You Loved the Fishermen
Characters

SPIRIT OF THE HURRICANE
PETER HAWKINS – a fisherman
JAMES – his son
SALOME – his wife
REBECCA – his daughter
JOHN – his nephew
LUCY ⎫
MARY ⎭ friends of Rebecca
MRS DAWS – a woman from a neighbouring village
CARRINGTON – a fisherman
Men and women of the village
Scene   A fishing beach in Tobago
Time   Early Monday morning, 30 September 1963

Prologue (*played in front of the curtain*)

*The stage is bare, the curtain closed. From behind the
curtain comes the sound of a group of voices singing:*

1 Johnny Grotto was a fisherman son
  yea, yea, yea ma boy
  Johnny Grotto was a fisherman son
  A long time ago.

2 He went out to sea to catch fishes for me
  yea, yea, yea ma boy.
  He went out to sea to catch fishes for me
  A long time ago.

3 The sea was so rough and the seine pulling tough,
  yea, yea, yea ma boy.
  The sea was so rough and the seine pulling tough,
  A long time ago.

4 He ketch plenty fish and he make a nice dish
  yea, yea, yea ma boy.
  He ketch plenty fish and he make a nice dish
  A long time ago.

*As soon as the singing stops, two heads emerge from the
middle of the curtain. They take a long look, with a
semicircular movement of the head scanning the audience,
then their figures appear from behind the curtain. They are
the Spirit of the Hurricane, a bi-sexual, composite
personality. The woman moves with exaggerated feminine
charm, the man with an arrogant virility in his gait. She
talks seductively, he talks blusteringly, and with an inflated
self-importance. They meet in the middle of the stage.*

MAN
For a start, they got my name wrong.

WOMAN
Because I have no name.

MAN
They called me Flora for convenience.

WOMAN
But that's excusable,
There' something very feminine about me.
I'm passionate and fierce, and men's dreams
Are nothing to me, neither are their schemes.

TOGETHER
I destroy them all.

MAN
They insult me when they give me only one name
Or only one sex, for that matter.

TOGETHER
*For I am all, and Both.
And my destruction knows no names, no categories.
I only destroy, I am very uncomplicated.*

MAN
Yes, I am a man too you know.
I have his muscles and his deadly unconcern
And remember, he has invented
Far worse things than me.

So as I am only an amateur
I will not contest him.

TOGETHER
I will only destroy him.

MAN
And then,
Only if he gets in my way.

TOGETHER
So you see, I am not vicious,
And he is of no real interest to me.

WOMAN
So, if I seem a little strange to you,
It is only because I am foreign,
And I haven't been a very frequent guest.

MAN
But I think you will remember me,
For I have a somewhat noticeable personality.
Shall we say I leave an impressive card,
Which I made available to all of you.

WOMAN
Tobago, you ask, 'Who sent me?
who dispatched me here?'

MAN
Well, that is not for me to say.

TOGETHER
But now I've come to watch this play,
To make sure that it gives no clues.
For I am possessive of my secrets.
Give me a chair.

He and she both click their fingers, and improvised seats are
brought on to both sides of the stage by grunting fishermen.
They take up their seats on either side of the stage and
remain there, scrutinizing the action, for the duration of
the play.

Scene 1

The curtain opens. The lights suggest a gradual sunrise. The lighted stage shows Hawkins, asleep in an apparent stupor, half in, half out of a small fishing boat, stage left. The setting is a beach, suggested by backcloth, nets, driftwood, palm branches, coconuts, sand and various items of flotsam. A rum bottle, empty of its contents, lies significantly beside Hawkins. John and James rush in, excited, bubbling.

JAMES Papa, Papa, ooooh Gosh, Papa.

JOHN Mr Hawkins, Mr Hawkins, wake up, Mr Hawkins.

JAMES Quick, Papa, the fish, the fish. (*He prods and pokes* Hawkins *who grunts and snorts. Then both boys pull* Hawkins *from the boat and drag him downstage.*) Plenty fishes, plenty fishes, so many fishes.

HAWKINS (Waking sluggishly) Wha' happen? Wha' happen? Wha' you doing? You madman boy? I' your father boy. You doesn't grab hold of my leg and pull me so.
(*He has a comatose expression, and makes uncoordinated attempts to grab his son. He speaks with a certain slur.*) Why you wake me like this? And me having a good sleep. Oooh God, your mother must have made a madman when she make you. Get out, get out, or I'll grab hold of you and cut all of you tail with blows. And you too young Webster, I see yo' father, I'll get he to beat you.

JAMES Noooh, Papa. Me no sick in me head, I no madman. It's the fish, get your net. Look, look at the sea. See the pelicans. See they diving all the time. It have a hundred pelicans out there, all diving and eating. (*Points straight at the audience, in the place of the sea.*) Look how fast they dive, oooh God, so quickly boy. They flash and they dive and then they go back for more. I never see they dive so quickly and so often. The sea is calm, but the big-ben and they dive so much, that they making their own waves.

HAWKINS Uuuhh?

JOHN And, Mr Hawkins, the fish, the little fish is
jumping like the sea too small fo' them, as if they is
being squashed out of the sea because they have no
room. Oooh, Mr Hawkins they is jumping, they is
jumping. It must have more fishes than water out there.
Go and get you' net, Mr Hawkins.

HAWKINS I never yet did cuss young children, but you
are bad, bad, worse than men. Making joke to me when
I is in this condition and I is sleeping good. I shall
cuss you so hard, and beat you boy if you don't give
me peace.

BOYS But, Papa . . . Mr Hawkins . . . I not lying, not
making joke . . . the fish, the fish.

HAWKINS Fish? Fish you say, boy? (*He speaks
ferociously, and the boys cower*) Boy, you has a hole
in you head? You has a big space boy? You vacant
there, eh, eh? Fish? You know boy, no fish here. De
fish gone away and they not coming by here again this
month. All day Friday, not fish boy, not a tail, not a
sprat. None Saturday too. Wha' you trying to tell me
boy? I get the man to look at you head. Oooh Lord, I
breed a lunatic for a son who run about with a set of
lunatic friends.

JAMES (*Indignant*) The big-ben were diving plenty
yesterday, I saw them.

HAWKINS Boy, I get him to look at you eyes too. Boy,
you knows that I don' fish on a Sunday. I let God
stock up he fishpond. I is a God-fearing man, I don' fish
no Sundays.

*Enter Salome and Rebecca. Salome walks fiercely across
the stage, Rebecca filters into the background. Salome is wild
and contemptuous. She sees Hawkins, and stamps up to
his prostrate form, glowering heavily.*

SALOME Well, look at you man, look at you. You have
a good rest eh? (*very sarcastically*) a good sleep? You
mattress nice and soft? You pillow keep your head
nice? You like the beach better than your home eh?

Better than me eh? I smell your tongue and you
mouth from here man. I set fire and put match to you'
breath. All of we go up bang. It blow up Tobago
man, all of we get blasted away.

HAWKINS Okay, okay, okay. I can't get no peace in the
place. My family 'sposed to look after me. Instead you
make my life misery. You does tear me 'part.

SALOME You drink up rum all afternoon and all
evening and all night, you lime all day and then sleep
in drunk sleep on the beach until the morning. You
'sposed to be a fisherman, but you doesn't pitch boat.
You doesn't mend net. You doesn't catch fish. You
does only catch rum, then you does drink it. You does
only drink like a fisherman. And now with all the
pelicans diving, and yesterday the little fish was all
jumping up like it was Carnival and they playing mas.

HAWKINS It don't have no fish this month I tell you.
De fish and them they gone away. And you know I
doesn't catch fish on Sundays. I let God stock up he
fishpond.

SALOME He fishpond, eh? He stock you up from his
rum-pond more like.

HAWKINS He will provide.

SALOME He provide you with rum. Why you always
bringing God into it. Why you always insult he by
making he defend you and what you do. Can you fish
on a Sunday? He say 'NO' you say. Can you drink rum
on a Sunday, all Sunday evening to Monday morning?
He say 'Yes' you say. Why you say that? Why you
always bringing he down to you lazy level. Why you
blame he, when you have the power to change you'
lazy self. I so vex with you.

HAWKINS (*Holding his head in desperation*) Woman,
woman, you stop getting at me, you hear? As soon as
the morning starts, you start too, and you does go on
until the day ends. You want to know why I does
drink rum? 'cause then I doesn't hear you so well.

SALOME You doesn't see so well either. You don't see

the fish when they is jumping up in front of you, right
up you' nose, saying you could get a good catch if you
wasn't the laziest man in Tobago.

Enter Mrs Daws at a run. She is flustered and puffing.

MRS DAWS Hawkins, man, Hawkins.

HAWKINS Good morning, Mrs Daws.

MRS DAWS Hawkins, man. Get out you' net.

HAWKINS You too, Mrs Daws? I thought you was a
friend of mine. De whol' world gone mad around me.
No peace, no peace.

MRS DAWS No man, I just come from round the rocks.
(*She gropes towards the boat and sits down.*) They get
a big, big catch in Grafton Bay. I seen they get whole
of Black Rock up there pulling seine. Sixty, seventy,
hundred people, right up the beach pulling that net.
Net full, full with jacks. No big fish, only jacks. Is
queer, Hawkins. The sea and them so calm, and yet the
little fish all swimming in shoals. Hundreds, thousands,
all come inside the bay. The water's thick, thick, solid
with jacks.

JAMES (*Proudly*) See, Papa, you did not breed lunatic
when you breed me. I right, I right.

JOHN (*Jumping up*) We right, we right.

MRS DAWS I never seen nothing like this, and all those
fishes, those little fishes. Everybody get bucket and
boxes and tins and pans and thing and them all
carrying them home. But, Hawkins, I never seen
nothing like those fishes. As they die, they is making a
funny, scary squeaky noise, and their eyes popping
right out of they sockets. And as they dying they
shaking and quivering and they is almost saying
something to you, as if they is warning you 'bout
something and they is really pleased. Is weird, is
strange man, Hawkins, I was scared studying them
fish die.

HAWKINS (*Reassuringly*) Tha's not strange. The little
fish, they does always act so. When they catch they
head in the net they does strangle in the twine. Then

they does choke like Hell, and they eyes come right
out, and look like they going to open out and bite you
all up.

MRS DAWS But they doesn't squeak like that man.
They not 'customed to make no noise usually, nothing
like that. Ther's millions of fishes out there, all making
that choke, that grate. I tell you they trying to tell de
fishermen something. They has a message, they all
choking in different sound and pitch. You hear it all
over the village.

SALOME (*Still aggressive*) You see what you missing by
lying here drinking plenty rum? Get the net in the sea
and catch me fish. You kids does need food, even if
you can live on rum.

HAWKINS Oooh God, dey says it have no rest for the
wicked. What I done eh? A good living man like
myself? Boy, boy, get me bucket of water boy.

Exit James in a hurry

*Hawkins staggers to his feet, looks towards the sea, rubs his
eyes and looks again.*

HAWKINS What? wha' happen? wha's going on?
Ooooh God, look at the pelicans. I can't see no sky, no
sea, no horizon only a set of birds in de place. There
is fish out there you know. There must be some fish?
what, de fish must be jumping from here to Trinidad?
Is that rum I been drinking, is that rum. I seeing things.
Is that rum. Boy, boy, is that rum I been drinking.

*Enter James, who staggers across the stage with a bucket of
water. Hawkins pours water over himself and looks again.*

What? They is still there.

SALOME You telling us news? You BBC? You Radio
Trinidad? You get transistor inside you' head?

HAWKINS Is a miracle I tell you. God has done a trick
for us. That's because I keep his holy day and show
respect see. You boy, get out the boat, and you Webster
get the nets out. And don't distract me woman wid you
talk. I have work to do.

Exit Hawkins with Boys in a hurry.

MRS DAWS Oooh Lord, the fish and them send everybody mad.

SALOME He always mad, he don't need no fish to be mad.

MRS DAWS You see how the sea is so calm, You ever seen it like that?

SALOME No I not studying the sea, look up there. There is big clouds in the distance, and the calm will soon go, and so will the fish. So he better get he nets quick, if he can move with all that rum inside he.

MRS DAWS Come, come I going to pull more seine, and make some grog for de fishermen. Oooh, the fish, the fish . . .

Exit Salome and Mrs Daws running.
The stage darkens and slides into grey, overcast gloom.
Rebecca, who has sat quietly at the back of the stage right through the scene, comes slowly forward, staring at the menacing sky on all sides. She shivers. She holds out her hand to find the rain. Then she moves off the stage with anxiety and trepidation.

Scene 2

Later that morning, same beach.
Enter Men and Women of the village. They are pulling in a seine net, and move stylistically across the stage from left to right to the accompaniment of African drums, singing, 'Johnny tief all the money. Pull away me boy'.
They exit. Then enter Rebecca and her friends Mary and Lucy. They are carrying buckets and tins filled with jacks. They are very exhilarated. Rebecca moves upstage.

LUCY We pull and we pull, Gul, but the net and them keep on snapping, but we caught plenty fishes you know.

MARY Everybody who pull carry home at least five bucketfuls.

LUCY But girl, why only the little ones? With all them jacks there should have been much bigger fishes. I don' understand. Not one redfish or carit or bonito or thing. The big fish should have been inside of the bay, having a big meal of the little fishes. Then we should have got them.

MARY Oooh, what you mean Lucy? You hush yo' mouth. You complaining when we have got all these fishes. We have fishes for a week in one catch, and you is ungrateful.

LUCY (*indignantly*) Me no moaning, and me no ungrateful. Gul, I just curious, that's all. I don' understand. There is always big fish when the little ones jumping, and yet they not here today. They must be out in the deeper water somewhere, or swimming under the rock. Why they not here then?

REBECCA (*Coming forward to front of the stage, in between Lucy and Mary*) I don't care why not. Girl I just grateful. You remember Sunday School yesterday? You remember the lesson? What the man say? How the fishermen, Peter and them, was fishing in the sea in Israel, and they was no fish? and they fish all day and still no fish? And then come Jesus and he say, 'what you men doing with no fish?' And Peter he say, 'the fish gone way sir, there no fish here today.' And so Jesus say to he, 'Put your nets over the other side of the boat.' So they do this, and, Gul, they get lots, lots, plenty, plenty, fish like we today. You hear the teacher yesterday, he say God loves the fisherman, like my Daddy. He love we, he love we, and so he fill we net for we.

MARY Yes. And them fishermen in the bible din' catch no carit or shark or any big fish you know girl. They was all small like our fish, because Jesus had to do miracle to make them feed the crowd. And a little boy carry them in he bag. So they was small girl.

LUCY Why yo' stupid Mary? It don't have shark in Israel. They only has little fish. We has much bigger fish in Tobago.

Exit Lucy.

REBECCA (*Looking to the sky, and putting out her hand*)
You feel rain? I think I felt a few spots, Gul. Look out
to sea, and up there over the fort. The sky is dark,
Gul, and behind them clouds is even blacker.

MARY (*Happily, as they wander off stage*) No matter, we
get enough. It can rain and blow for weeks if it want.

*Exit Mary and Rebecca, downstage left. As they move off
enter Hawkins and Carrington, both slightly drunk, leaning
on each other. They sing 'Rum Glorious Rum, when I call
you you bound to come'.*

HAWKINS What you think about all this, Carrie? All
them jacks, and them so contorted and scared and
choking. They not 'customed to die so, you know.

CARRINGTON Well, Mr Hawkins, me no question this.
Everything come to he who wait. We done we waiting
all last week, and now is time for them to come to we.
Is not before time, Mr Hawkins, we been good, patient
men, and now is we due. It don't have nothing strange,
nothing sinister, Mr Hawkins, we been good, patient
christian men. (*He opens a rum bottle that he holds in
his hand*) You like a little drink, a little swig. I think
we found good reason to spread joy. I never caught so
many jacks before.

HAWKINS (*with an affected reluctance*) Yes, sir, I will
take a drop, although is bad for me during the week.
I don't normally touch it during the week. You know
that, Carrie.

CARRINGTON Yes of course, yes of course, man. You
is a Saturday man, and then you is wild.

HAWKINS (*His ego flattered*) Well, I hope I is a man,
flesh and blood, Carrie, and I has my little weakness
and indulgences in moderation, of course, Carrie.

CARRINGTON (*Humouring him*) Of course, yes of
course. You is right. That's the word, Mr Hawkins,
Moderation. You have another swig, Mr Hawkins, as
a celebration of course, Mr Hawkins.

HAWKINS As a celebration, as an occasion, Carrie, I will
take one. I always say the bounds of moderation is

always increased, Carrie, when it have occasion.

CARRINGTON True again, Mr Hawkins. I always says
an occasion make 'e own rule, otherwise it wouldn't
be an occasion.

HAWKINS (*Taking the rum as Carrington is drinking*)
Right again, Carrie, right again. (*In the background
begins a slow throbbing beat of African drums, quiet at
first but gradually getting louder.*) Carrie, you is a wise
man. You has no education, no school education like
me, because you never went to Bishops. But you is a
wise man.

CARRINGTON The winds is getting high, Mr Hawkins.
You think we in for a storm? Is been hot last week.

HAWKINS Is good to have a purge now and then.
Washes we out a little. I calls it a purge, Carrie, a
purge. Like someone pull on the chain on we and
wash we down. We is sinners all, Carrie, and we need
to be washed out now and then. Is good for us.

CARRINGTON That is right, Mr Hawkins, that is right.
My ol' man in Scarboro' he used to say that when the
rains wash we down and beat on the galvanize like it
were machine gun. He used to stand out in the rain
and make us do it too, and he say to we, to my brother
and my little sisters and me, he say, 'Boys, and
Victorine' – that's my little sister, she gone up
Charlotteville now, 'This is good for you,' he say, 'you
feel God direct,' he say. 'This is good for you, it teach
you humility.'

HAWKINS That's something we all need, Carrie, that's
something we all need. (*Finishes the rum and throws
down the bottle; there is a loud burst of drumming.*)
This is a high wind, Carrie. It is a big one. You see
that cloud up there over the fort? What she remind
you of? (*The stage gradually darkens.*)

CARRINGTON (*Unconcerned*) Like a cloud, just a cloud
man, a very dark one, but just a cloud.

HAWKINS Look good, man, look good. I mean the
shape. You got no power for seeing shapes, Carrie.

You not an artist like me. You not got the imagination
man, not like me. I see patterns everywhere.

CARRINGTON Is the rum, Mr Hawkins. You seeing thing
because of the rum. That Bajan rum is good and strong.

HAWKINS (*Annoyed*) I can take me liquor, man, I can
take me rum. I don't see things that arn' there. You
know that, Carrie. I is a good, hard drinker.

CARRINGTON Of course yes, Mr Hawkins of course.

HAWKINS (*Looking up at the sky*) I don' like that cloud,
and is creeping up. Is like a gundy, Carrie, a big crab
gundy, and we is right between the pinchers (*He makes
a significant gesture. By this time the stage has
darkened over completely and Hawkins and Carrington
are mere silhouettes.*) Is coming right towards us.

CARRINGTON You need some mo' rum man, we go and
get another bottle.

HAWKINS Not now man, doesn't you study anything
else? Them jacks is good and fresh. We go and have
a cook.

CARRINGTON Yes, yes, man.

HAWKINS But I don't like that crab gundy. Is ugly,
Carrie, very ugly. I think we in for a big storm. I
worried for my little girl in we old house. (*He
considers*) If de storm get really bad boy, I send my
daughter into the church, she is going to be safe there
boy, that's the safest place. Come on man we go
and eat.

Crashing of drums suggesting the approaching hurricane.

Scene 3

*The hurricane in all its fury. The stage is empty. The lights
flash on and off. Upstage various missiles are being hurled
on the centre of the stage: from the wings come palm
branches, coconuts, sheets of galvanize, piping, wood,
buckets, etc. Accompanying this clatter is frantic, discordant
drumming and screams and moans from the wings. Figures
rush on from both sides of the stage in stylized attitudes of*

*terror and fear. They fight against the wind and the noise
and stagger and flounder around the stage, shouting 'My
house, my house', or 'My child, my child' or 'The school, the
school.' They exit. As the noise increases a Man and a
Woman stagger on to the stage. As they shout the drumming
stops, but continues ferociously for five-second intervals
between each line. They face the audience in horror,
supporting each other. Stylized speech.*

MAN The sea, the sea, it boils like broth, it knows no
calm.

WOMAN The trees and branches blow around my eyes,
all roots are gone.

MAN See, see the sky. See the balls of woollen wind as
they scream towards us.

WOMAN Feel the frown of God.

MAN Hear the cries of men.

WOMAN See their houses fly.

MAN And their children die.

WOMAN Hear the animals screech.

TOGETHER As we all reach, reach, reach, reach towards
you God.

*Exit fighting against the wind, struggling to keep their feet.
More frantic drumming and hurling, with flashing lights.
Enter another Woman, floundering on the stage. Between
every phrase she speaks is a short clip from the drums.*

2ND WOMAN The church! the church! The church is
down. It smashed and it fell. Who was inside? Who
was inside? I saw the wood break and the beams fall.
Then the galvanize flew all around and cut the air and
plunged into the church. I heard the crash and felt
huge wounds. I felt my own flesh break and flow. Who
was inside? Who was inside?

*She exits. More cacophony. Then from the back of the stage
enter Hawkins. He is carrying the motionless Rebecca in his
arms, and he fights clownishly against the vortex. He is
crying in absolute grief and perplexity. He comes to the
front centre of the stage, lays down Rebecca, and kneels
behind her.*

HAWKINS Why? Why? It should have been the safest
place. I told her to go there. I told her to go there. How
could I know? What can I know? What did she know?
What did she think? Who knows? Who thinks? O
Jesus, Jesus, I thought you was a friend of the
fishermen. O God I thought you loved the fishermen . . .
*Hawkins picks up Rebecca, with the help of Carrington who
has emerged from the darkness at the back of the stage.
Hawkins seems about to speak again. But at that moment
the Spirit of the Hurricane rises suddenly from both sides of
the stage, and man figure places his hand over Hawkins's
mouth, stopping any more words, freezing the characters,
and stopping all the noise. Hawkins and Carrington
carrying Rebecca, gradually move backwards upstage and
the curtain closes on them. The Spirit of the Hurricane
relaxes in front of the curtain.*

Epilogue

MAN Well that really got quite earnest, didn't it?
WOMAN But I won't say how warm.
MAN You know, sometimes I can feel quite guilty
When I see what I do.
And yet, like most of you, I only do a job.
And after all, I would never blame you for that,
So would you blame me?
TOGETHER *Remember, I have no malice.
So please don't think me too despicable.*
WOMAN I know that we can never be friends,
But that is no reason for us to be enemies.
MAN You see, I cannot help my own nature, neither
Can you help yours, and I don't hate you.
In fact, I must admit that sometimes . . .
TOGETHER *I quite admire your heroism.*
WOMAN So don't spoil things and embarrass me, by
asking, 'who sent me', 'who is my chief?' because
awkward silences spoil any new relationship.
TOGETHER *And I can tell you nothing.*

MAN Don't ask me if I come from God

WOMAN Or Satan

MAN Or Nature

WOMAN Or Mohammed

MAN Or from the sins of man.

TOGETHER *Just know me and remember what I look like.*
    Remember my face.

They deliberately show their faces to the audience in
histrionic gestures.

WOMAN Then, if I ever come again, then . . .
    Well, perhaps we can meet on a more cordial basis.

BOTH *Thank you for the chair.*

MAN By the way – Do I get a present for coming?
    Ha ha.

WOMAN Well, perhaps next time – Ummmh?

In the background there is singing. AZA BUIL' WA
NEW BOAT.

MAN And please don't call me Flora. (*Indignant*)
    It really does sound a little too intimate,
    Almost if you liked me.

WOMAN And I'm quite sure you don't feel that affectionate
    Towards me.

Man raises his hand to his ear.

MAN Well, listen to them now. Singing very nicely.
    They soon got over us, didn't they?

WOMAN They will soon be happy again. It is amazing.
    I will never understand them.

BOTH Well, sleep well. (*Pause*) I may not bother you.

MAN Goodnight ladies.

WOMAN Goodnight gentlemen.

They exit behind the curtain, the singing goes on.

Concluding song:

1 Aza buil' wa new boat
    Aza buil' wa new boat
    Aza buil' wa new boat
    An' 'e call am Tobago massa.

Chorus:
> Goodbye Aza, Goodbye – O
> Goodbye Aza, Goodbye – O
> Goodbye O' mi baby,
> An' 'e call am Tobago massa.

2 Aza ketch one big fish
  Aza ketch one big fish
  Aza ketch one big fish
  An' 'e call am Tobago massa.

3 Aza cook one sweet pot,
  Aza cook one sweet pot,
  Aza cook one sweet pot,
  An' 'e call am Tobago massa.

4 Aza take one big sleep,
  Aza take one big sleep,
  Aza take one big sleep,
  An' 'e call am Tobago massa.

7 After awareness

There is no turning back from awareness.[1]

George Jackson

Awareness of the ideas in this account can only bring discomfort. There is nothing to feel satisfied in what the white man's words are doing to black people. But to merely raise children's consciousness to an awareness of alienation and discomfort is a futile and evil process, unless it is accompanied with some answers or commitments to alternatives. For George Jackson the awareness brought its torment and desperation:

Why can't I rid myself of the sorrow and emotion
that awareness has brought me? I get rid of the
self-destructive force of error and ignorance only to be
torn and miserable by what I discover.[2]

It was only an active and complete revolt against his accepted identity given to him by his mother and his country that caused him to find love and discovery. He would not serve white words and images:

For you there is only one standard of beauty, the Western
standard. I revolt against this absurdity. I understand that
this is all you have ever known, I allow for this, but you
must be able to see by now that this model of perfection
you have subscribed to in the past is no longer the fad.
Black is black. I'm going to fulfil my role as a man, even
if it kills me.[3]

We know that this absurdity is not only the state of a black man living in a white man's world. We are all living in a society which divides us from each other, causes distrust, fear and loneliness. The black man's state is only one image of ourselves. We have poems, novels, plays that speak of a deep awareness of our absurdity and alienation, but where do we go from there? Having accepted his own particular image of absurdity, how does the black man act? How do any of us act?

There is a section in Mayhew's *London Labour and the London Poor*, published in 1851, where the author interviews a black beggar on the streets in Whitechapel.[4] 'Ladies give me halfpence oftener than men,' says the black man. 'The butchers call me Othello and ask me why I killed my wife.' And still today, the white man's commentary on the black man is often only a predictable cluster of clichés. Now if a West Indian immigrant, walking up the Mile End Road, should look up at the sign of the public house next to Stepney Green Station, he will see 'The Black Boy'. He will see himself in a turban with a white feather, wearing a hanoverian flared coat, yellow stockings, lace cravat and cuffs, and black shoes with shining buckles. He will see himself with wheyed face, carrying a tray with a porcelain jug on it. He will see what the white man has done to his identity, and what he is still doing. The black man must take command of his own identity. He cannot trust the white man and his culture to organize and portray his life for him. Ways have to be found so that the black child, whether he lives in the Caribbean, or whether he lives in Britain, can speak for himself and his own life without having to adopt white forms and values. He must grow up with his identity intact, unbetrayed. He must have control over his own personal and social growth. Jackson wrote to his mother:

You have been failed, by history and events, and people over whom you had no control. Only after you understand this can you then go and make the necessary alterations that will bring some purpose and value to your life; you must gain some control.[5]

A dynamic movement towards more social control for black people in England has come to Bernard Coard's book for the Caribbean Education and Community Workers' Association, *How the West Indian Child is made Educationally Sub-normal in the British School System*. Coard demonstrates how British white middle-class culture pressurizes the black immigrant child to hate his own blackness, refuse to admit it, and makes him rather see himself as white: 'the children are therefore made neurotic about their race and culture'. Everything in their social world speaks against their blackness:

The black child's true identity is denied daily in the classroom. In so far as he is given an identity, it is a false one...*

If every reference on TV, radio, newspapers, reading books and story books in school shows 'black' as being horrible and ugly, and everything 'white' as being pure, clean and beautiful, then people begin to think this way on racial matters.[6]

Coard tells his readers that 'pride and self-confidence' are what is needed by the black man faced with the pressures of white culture. He emphasizes the need for black community action, more parental control over education, black nursery schools and supplementary schools, Caribbean syllabuses, more West Indian teachers, investigations into IQ tests and streaming systems which favour whites, and an end to placing West Indian children in educationally sub-normal

* This process happens from the earliest acquisition of language in the schools. The 'Peter and Jane' Ladybird primers, used extensively in junior schools with a high proportion of Caribbean working-class children, include their first black faces as a golliwog and a black doll with straightened hair and lipstick) when blonde, white middle-class Jane goes into a toyshop. The same publisher's 'easy-reading' *Beauty and the Beast* has, predictably, a white, blonde Beauty and a black ape-like Beast, who turns into a handsome white prince when Beauty shows her goodness to him. At one point, the Beast asks, 'Am I very ugly, Beauty,' and Beauty answers, 'Yes, Beast.'

schools until they have had a minimum of two years in a
normal school.

Black people living in white societies or societies afflicted
by a legacy of colonialism are beginning to deal very radi-
cally with their cultural absurdity. They are making their
insights known through their own presses and community
newspapers. They know that the old domination and be-
trayal need to be completely removed. They are creating
new directions, new beginnings:

What we have to create is a new man; a man who
masters himself and his environment; a man who
combines mental and physical labour and a man who in
his daily actions can give free expression to his many
and varied talent and capacities.[7]

The awareness and recognition of themselves as prisoners
of white culture and language is causing them to act in a
stronger and more unified way to free themselves. This becomes everyone's struggle. It is a forerunner of any movement by any people under cultural and political domination
towards social health and control over their own lives:

All living in one community
Thinking for each other
Helping each other
No betrayals.[8]

References

Introduction

1. Derek Walcott, 'Laventville', *The Castaway*, Cape, 1965, p. 33.
2. Frantz Fanon, *Black Skin White Masks*, Paladin, 1970, pp. 61, 165.
3. *Childhood and Society*, Penguin, 1965, p. 241.
4. Ralph Ellison, quoted in John Dixon's *Growth through English*, Oxford University Press, 1967, p. 19.
5. Fanon, op. cit., p. 27.

1 Monostatus

1. Frantz Fanon, *Black Skin White Masks*, Paladin, 1970, pp. 14, 16, 12, 26, 38.
2. ibid., p. 99.
3. *Journal of Black Poetry* (winter–spring 1970), ed. Askia Muhammed Touré, vol. 1, no. 13, p. 100.
4. *Soledad Brother*, Penguin, 1971, pp. 61, 62, 97, 112.
5. Fanon, op. cit., p. 165.

2 The island theme

1. Cheryl Fraser, 'Self portrait', *Children as Writers*, Daily Mirror Press, p. 42.
2. P. B. Shelley, 'Lines Written among the Euganean Hills', *Selected Poems* (ed. E. Blunden), Collins, 1954, p. 151.
3. Derek Townsend, *Caribbean Guide*, Allen & Unwin, 1970, p. 47.
4. Lord Kitchener, 'Ode to Tobago', *King of the Road*, Tropico Records, Port of Spain, 1969.

5. J. M. Cohen (ed.), *The Four Voyages of Christopher Columbus*, Penguin, 1969, p. 221.

3 Language and identity

1. Penguin, 1969, p. 182.
2. *The Politics of Experience*, Penguin, 1969, p. 53.
3. 'Codicil', *The Castaway*, Cape, 1965, p. 61.
4. B. Bernstein and D. Henderson, 'Social class differences in the relevance of language to socialization', *Sociology*, vol. 3, no. 1.
5. *West Indian Children in London*, Bell, 1967, p. 31.
6. *The Times Educational Supplement*, 20 March 1970, p .20.
7. Frantz Fanon, *The Wretched of the Earth*, Penguin, 1968, p. 314.
8. Edward Brathwaite, 'Caliban', *Islands*, Oxford University Press, 1969, p. 35.
9. *The Tempest*, Act I, Scene 2.
10. Act I, Scene 5.
11. *The Winter's Tale*, Act IV, Scene 3.
12. *Othello*, Act I, Scene 1.

4 English against identity

1. Stanley Hewitt (ed.), *This Day and Age*, Arnold, 1960, p. 49.
2. Kenneth Ramchand (ed.), *West Indian Narrative*, Nelson, 1966, p. 102.
3. ibid., Introduction, p. 10.
4. ibid., p. 2.
5. Collins, 1963, p. 469.
6. ibid., p. 209.
7. Penguin, 1966, p. 60.
8. Derek Walcott, 'November Sun', *The Castaway*, Cape, 1965, p. 45.
9. Stanley Hewitt (ed.), *This Day and Age*, Arnold, 1960, p. 60.
10. Aimé Césaire (trans. J. Berger and A. Bostock), *Return to My Native Land*, Penguin, 1965, p. 63.

5 **English for identity?**

1. Edward Brathwaite, 'Epilogue', *Rights of Passage*, Oxford University Press, 1967, p. 86.

2. Michael Joseph, 1963, p. 36.

3. From Jonathan Kozol, *Death at an Early Age*, Penguin, 1968, p. 189.

4. Trinidad and Tobago Arts Festival Association, *Arts Festival Syllabus*, 1969, p. 17.

5. ibid., p. 28.

6. Government of Trinidad and Tobago, *Draft Plan for Educational Development in Trinidad and Tobago, 1968–1983*, Port of Spain, Government Printery, 1968, p. 35.

7. op. cit., p. 78.

8. ibid., p. 33.

9. Jean Rhys, *Voyage in the Dark*, Penguin, 1969, p. 7.

10. V. S. Naipaul, *An Area of Darkness*, Penguin, 1968, p. 27.

11. Penguin, 1969, p. 207.

12. Penguin, 1969, p. 75.

13. Kenneth Ramchand (ed.), *West Indian Narrative*, Nelson, 1966, p. 1.

14. Edward Brathwaite, 'Legba', *Islands*, Oxford University Press, 1969, p. 15.

15. *The Merchant of Venice*, Act II, Scene 1.

16. Coleridge, *The Ancient Mariner*.

6 **Drama and identity**

1. Frantz Fanon, *Black Skin White Masks*, Paladin, 1970, p. 158.

2. Frantz Fanon, *The Wretched of the Earth*, Penguin, 1968, p. 315.

3. Edward Brathwaite, 'Wake', *Islands*, Oxford University Press, 1969, p. 55.

4. Edward Brathwaite, 'Negus', *Islands*, pp. 66–7.

7 After awareness

1. *Soledad Brother*, Penguin, 1971, p. 139.
2. ibid., p. 84.
3. ibid., p. 165.
4. Peter Quennell (ed.), *Mayhew's Characters*, Spring Books, 1950, p. 391.
5. *Soledad Brother*, p. 67.
6. New Beacon Books, 1971, pp. 30, 28, 29, 39.
7. *New Beginning*, vol. 1, no. 5, San Fernando, Trinidad, 2 April 1971.
8. Maxine McCarthy, 'Racial harmony' in *Stepney Words Number 2*, Reality Press, 1971, p. 7.